MAY - - 2016

CRUSH

WILLIAM MORROW *An Imprint of* HarperCollins*Publishers*

CRUSH

WRITERS
REFLECT on LOVE,
LONGING,
and the LASTING
POWER of
THEIR FIRST
CELEBRITY
CRUSH

CATHY ALTER and **DAVE SINGLETON**

FIRST EDITION

Designed by Fritz Metsch

Library of Congress Cataloging-in-Publication Data has been applied for.

ISBN 978-0-06-239955-7

16 17 18 19 20   OV/RRD   10 9 8 7 6 5 4 3 2 1

Cathy dedicates this book to Susan, her cherished mother, who taught her that a trip to Manhattan was never complete without a celebrity spotting.

Dave dedicates this book to Bobbi Whalen and Christina Rudolph, without whose love, devotion, "muse-ing," laughs, and late-night/early-morning phone calls, there'd be no book (or much else good, for that matter).

Contents

Introduction

First crushes are enduring. It doesn't matter how old you are now, there's still an indelible image—the boy who sat behind you in math class, the girl who lived next door, every junior counselor at your summer camp—etched into your memory.

Throw a celebrity into the mix and there's a whole new level of potency. Maybe it was David Cassidy making you feel like you didn't just *think* you loved him—you knew. Perhaps you stared at Farrah Fawcett and her red-swimsuit poster on your wall until you were convinced she was the only girl for you.

Both painfully real and wholly implausible, your first celebrity crush is a hormonal alchemy capable of producing—as evidenced on the pages to follow—poignant and funny stories that say much more about the admirer than the admired.

Celebrity crushes change and mold us into the people we will become, shaping our ideals, fueling our fantasies, aiding and abetting our conquests, and leading us to (or away from) the people we meet and fall in love with decades later.

Celebrities are our ideals in love, our best friends, our parental proxies, and more. They give us hope—that we are lovable, popular, and gorgeous enough (as, ahem, one of us here once believed) for Sting to definitely spot us in the nosebleed section of Madison Square Garden.

They offered us safe places—on the pages of *Teen Beat* magazine, in a darkened movie theater, or in front of the TV, nestled in a family of Partridges—where we could try on and try out feelings. Removed from the anxiety of actually having to talk to these gods and goddesses, we could instead dream up conversations while staring at their images plastered to our bedroom walls.

As one of our brilliant contributors writes: "What else is a crush but a repository for our own passions and unfulfilled real-life relationships?"

And that is the role that celebrities play. They are both knowable yet distant; familiar and remote. It is this dichotomy that produces intense desire, but also, because our passions are never returned, we must eventually deal with crushing disappointment. And so we move on.

Whether we feel the pull eight-year-old Stephen King felt seeing screen siren Kim Novak for the first time or empathize with Jodi Picoult's crush on Donny Osmond, we understand their longing. Our parents may have called our first celebrity crushes "puppy love," but for us these crushes were our earliest approximation of love and demanded to be taken seriously.

Sometimes our first celebrity crushes are the people we want to become. Ballet legend Mikhail Baryshnikov led Kimberly Dawn Neumann to dance, and cartoon character Speed Racer turned Jamie Brisick into a champion surfer. James Franco saw in River Phoenix both the young man and the actor he wanted to become.

This book started with the two of us talking about our celebrity crushes, Donny Osmond and David Cassidy. The more we explored the origins of our crushes, the more we realized how much these celebrities had influenced us and how our stories were deeper than just fleeting fancy. Which led us to wonder who influenced some of our own literary crushes. How did their crushes affect them and what did they think about them long after the initial crush subsided?

To find our contributors we turned to the eternal question that Bo Diddley put to music: "Who do you love?" Thirty-eight of our favorites have shared with us their most profound first crushes. They bring together emotional heft, brilliant wordplay, and deep insights into what it means to love someone with such one-sided fervor. Some contributors, like James Franco and Andrew McCarthy, have been the object of crushes and, in writing their essays, have turned the tables on themselves.

For us, the variety of voices and the depth of their prose achieve remarkable sweep and power. By including writers of various ages, ethnicities, orientations, and experiences, the essays examine how crushee and crusher reflect the era in which they were born.

The stories, while sometimes subtle, still manage to illuminate the social conventions and consciousness of the times. While it's true that millions universally adored pop culture icons from Marilyn Monroe to Brad Pitt, the stories of our crushes are unique to each storyteller.

Even if you weren't in love with Jared Leto like former *Gawker*-ette Emily Gould, the ability to relate, to share, to commiserate, to understand, is affirming. We've all been there, whether your "there" was a superhero or, in the case of Andrew McCarthy, his worship of (and sexual awakening to) a super body.

If, as the late anthropologist Clifford Geertz suggested, culture can be summed up as an "ensemble of stories we tell about ourselves," these crushes, like prehistoric insects trapped in amber, remind us of who we were, in all our brace-faced, unencumbered glory, when anything and everything was both possible and futile.

PART 1

My Idol

Icons and idols cut across generations, with heartthrobs in every decade, from James Dean and Marilyn Monroe all the way to current crushes like Harry Styles and Rihanna. These crushes reflect pop culture time capsules, bottling both the era and the crush forever.

JODI PICOULT

And They Called It Puppy Love

I was six years old, and I was running away from home.

Angry and teary in the aftermath of a lightning bolt of discipline that had been hurled by my mother, I stuffed a toothbrush, a hairbrush, and a change of clothes into my pillowcase. I scrawled a note for my mother and left it on my bureau. Then I sneaked downstairs and slipped out the back door into the smothering heat of an August night, intent on running away to be with the one person I was certain would appreciate me.

The note read: *I have gone to live with Donny Osmond. Don't try to come after me.*

I can't tell you what it was about Donny that captured me at such a young age. Maybe it was the incandescent gleam of his perfect teeth, or the seventies swoop of hair across his brow. Maybe it was the way he teased his sister, Marie, on television every week on their variety show, with canned jokes that were actually funny to someone under the age of ten. Maybe it was his cover photo on *Teen Beat,* which I had clutched so often it was creased and faded at the edges. Maybe it was the records I spun over and over on my little portable player. Lying on my belly, chin propped in my hands, I'd belt along to "Puppy Love." And when Donny sang "Go Away Little Girl," I knew he was crooning exclusively to me.

My parents thought my obsession was cute—so much so that for my sixth birthday they presented me with The Best Gift Ever: a Donny Osmond pillowcase. It was white and purple and featured a grainy photograph of Donny's beaming face, along with the words "SWEET DREAMS." Every night after my parents tucked me in and gently closed my bedroom door, I'd sit up and cradle the pillowcase in my arms. I'd kiss Donny the way I saw adults kiss on television: eyes closed, lips pressed tight.

The night I ran away from home, of course, I took my Donny Osmond pillowcase. I slung it over my shoulder, feeling the sharp edges of the life I was leaving behind as the contents bounced against the small of my back. I crept past the barbecue and considered hiding underneath the cover, but it was too hot. I settled for scrambling on my hands and knees beneath a row of hedges that backed up to the fence in our tiny backyard. It was the same place I went when I was playing at being a spy, and when I wanted to collect acorns and twigs to make houses for fairies. In the cool shade, I smoothed the pillowcase over my lap, touching Donny's inked purple cheek. I didn't have a valid plan, mind you. I was barely in elementary school and had no idea where Donny Osmond lived, what his beliefs were, what he would make of a six-year-old girl with a wickedly fierce crush on him. But that was exactly *why* I loved him. I knew nothing about who the object of my affection was in his real life. He was, purely and simply, what I needed him to be in *mine:* A wish. A way to pretend to be older than I actually was. A perfectly safe relationship, because it was completely one-sided.

Crushes are love for the fainthearted, a way to practice pairing up before the stakes get intense. Much like the way a little girl delights in putting on makeup with her mom long before she is old enough to actually start wearing it, or how she swaddles and feeds a doll decades before having a baby of her own, role-playing at love is a dress rehearsal, a trial run before you give your heart to someone. A crush—by definition—will never hurt you, not as long as you've invented him correctly, building him up to dynamic and unrealistic proportions in your mind. On the other hand, a real romantic relationship is a bottomless black pit into which you dive blindly—sometimes you hit the water, sometimes you land on the rocks. It's so much easier to adore someone imaginary. My husband told me once that when he was thirteen, he dreamed he was crazy in love with a girl named Sandra. He could still, years later, describe the color of her hair and her lopsided smile and the way she smelled like sunlight and apples. Before he woke up, Sandra turned into a rabbit and hopped away from him. For weeks, he was moody and depressed, even though the girl he'd lost had never been real.

True, Donny Osmond *was* real, but that hardly compared to the version of him I'd created in my mind's eye. To me he was not a Mormon or an entertainer. I did not even really see him as a teenager—although he was the same age as the boy who lived across the street, who had sideburns and armpit hair and was rumored to have made out with a substitute teacher behind the wood shop at the high school. No, in my dreams, Donny was clean-cut and asexual, attentive and gentle and understanding. I've sometimes wondered what would have happened if I'd magically teleported from my backyard that evening to the studio where *Donny & Marie* was filmed, what Mr. Osmond would have done when confronted by a grubby, tear-stained child clutching a pillowcase emblazoned with a bad likeness of his face. I like to think that with his many siblings and cousins, he would have been kind. I like to believe he would have given me a cookie to feed my hunger, and perhaps a kiss on the cheek to feed my dreams.

Many years later, I had the chance to watch Donny Osmond perform in *Joseph and the Amazing Technicolor Dreamcoat*. By now we were both adults with families of our own. He sang from the bottom of his soul—not the bubblegum pop that had made me adore him as a child, but a tortured ballad about what it feels like to have everything taken away from you. He was half-naked onstage, and I was now old enough to appreciate his physical attractiveness, and to feel the embers of that old crush start to burn in a new, corporeal way. *What if . . . ?* I thought, for all of half a second. It was not completely unlikely that his wife or sons or daughters-in-law—or even Donny himself—might have stumbled over one of my books and enjoyed it. Because of Hollywood and Broadway adaptations of my work, there was even a slight, odd chance that we might one day meet. But what would happen if the crush collided with the real man?

I have heard, from people who've met Donny Osmond, that he is a nice guy. There is a lot we have in common now that we might talk about—a dedication to family, an unflagging work ethic. But there are significant points of disagreement, too—due to his faith, Donny allegedly opposes same-sex marriage and sees homosexuality as a personal choice; I believe homosexuality is not a decision that's made by an individual but simply the way some folks are wired, and I am happily planning my gay son's upcoming wedding. Ultimately, this is the reason crushes don't become true loves: reality is messy, and people rarely turn out to be the people we wish them to be. If I ever *do* meet Donny Osmond, I'll be charming. I will tell him about that pillowcase, which I kept until it was threadbare. I'll thank him for being my first love. But I will also be silently grateful he was not my last—that instead, I found a guy who was the man not just of my dreams but of my reality.

One month after I packed up my pillowcase to go live with Donny Osmond, I started first grade. There, I met a boy named Kal who had a jungle gym in his basement and a pet iguana in a tank in his bedroom. Kal also had shaggy, leonine hair and a smile that unspooled like ribbon. If love, at age six, means sliding down the staircase on gym mats and sharing your Rice Krispies Treats . . . then I fell madly, truly, deeply.

But what actually happened on that lazy summer night, when I ran away to live with Donny Osmond? Well, I stayed hidden for about forty-five minutes, until my mother fired up the barbecue and the backyard grew thick with the scent of buttery corn on the cob, of sputtering hamburgers. I crawled out of my hiding place in time for dinner. While I ate, my mother took my pillowcase upstairs and slipped it back onto my pillow. She folded my shorts and my shirt and my underwear and tucked them into their respective drawers. She put my toothbrush and my hairbrush in the bathroom.

My mother never made fun of me for wanting to run off with Donny Osmond, something for which I am eternally grateful.

But then again, I have it on good authority that, once, *she* had a wicked crush on Paul Anka.

STEPHEN KING

Beautiful

My first celebrity crush was Kim Novak, in *Picnic*. There is a scene where she and William Holden stare at each other, clapping their hands to some fairly hot music. They don't dance, just clap and stare. What was I doing in that movie theater, watching that movie? I can't remember, but someone must have just hauled me along. One of my aunts, maybe, stuck on babysitting duty.

Novak was so heavy-eyed and feral. It was the first time I really noticed a woman's breasts, I think—at least coupled to a desire to touch them. I fell deeply in love, although she was adult and terrifying. I could imagine a kiss from her as being a prelude to ingesting me whole, but that would have been okay. Just fine, in fact.

I measured beauty by Kim Novak for years. Some girls were beautiful and some were desirable, but none of them combined the two in such a volatile mix. I have just checked on the web, and that movie was released in 1955, which would have made me just eight.

I've Got a Crush on Julia Roberts . . . and Six Words

We gush when we crush on celebrities. I know I do. Julia Roberts? I can safely say my wife doesn't need to hear another word about her. But six words? That she can handle. And, really, what more do you need to know about Julia and me than "It was love at first slice"? (Well, it was the eighties. *Mystic Pizza* was a seminal movie in my young life . . .)

Taking a page from Ernest Hemingway, who, legend has it, wrote a whole novel in just six words ("For sale: Baby shoes, never worn"), I'm hooked on boiling things down to their essence.

The essence of Six-Word Memoirs is to get to the heart of who you are and what matters most in a half-dozen carefully selected words. The best six-word stories come from a place of passion. And it's no surprise that feeling starstruck leads to passionate Six'ing.

If you're out there, Julia, here are six more words: "I've got a crush on you."

The Winners from Smith Magazine's Six-Word Celebrity Crush Contest

Since we wanted to find some of the best new Six-Word Memoirs and include them in our book, Larry Smith created the Six-Word Celebrity Crush Contest, launching it on his website SixWordMemoirs.com. He asked his readers to tell us which celebrities first captured their hearts and sparked their imaginations.

The result? Six-Word Memoirs came pouring in with heart, soul, and brevity. As this selection of the best entries reveals, those early passions can be reignited in an instant (or in just six words).

Penélope Cruz: My Woman on Top. —Guy Austin
Oh to be Mr. Darcy's shirt. (Colin Firth) —Amy Nealon
My *Tiger Beat* centerfold first kiss. (Shaun Cassidy)
 —Amy Smith Pickett
From sneakers to crop tops. Sigh. (Taylor Swift)
 —Jean Stanula
At 21 I jumped, never descending. (Johnny Depp)
 —Hillary Nichols
Love the rock, he told me. (Albert Camus) —Lorraine Berry
Drive me but, I'm no Daisy. (Morgan Freeman)
 —Kyoka Akers
Heaven Can Wait. I'd rather not. (Warren Beatty)
 —Susan Breeden
Her tight dress improved my circulation. (Morticia Addams)
 —Dan Campbell
He was hot as his sauce. (Paul Newman) —Zsuzsanna Kis
Had my heart at first bite. (Bela Lugosi as Dracula)
 —Leslie Long
9 0 2 1 Oh Dylan. (Luke Perry) —Jackie Leventhal
Dave Grohl. Dave Grohl. Dave Grohl. —Tara Dublin
Are you coming to my dinner. (Sidney Poitier)
 —Jo Ann Daniels
Still makes being different feel delightful. (Morrissey)
 —Lisa Carlson
Battling with daughter over Bradley Cooper!
 —Linda Maxwell
He left me shaken and stirred. (Sean Connery)
 —Beverly Virginia Head

Of course I like them apples. (Matt Damon)
—Chelsey Drysdale
Always wanted to be Jessie's girl. (Rick Springfield)
—Rachell Summers
Duckie. *Pretty in Pink.* Quirky hotness. (Jon Cryer)
—Kimberly Ann Payne
Boy crushes only, until Julia Roberts. —Sana Lynn
My tastes have improved since then. (Vanilla Ice)
—Kellie Fournier
My illogical heart belongs to Spock. —Neesha Hosein
"Dear Emma," Redacted. "Dear Unrequited Feelings."
(Emma Watson) —Jarrett Dykes
Men who dance: Baryshnikov, Travolta, Walken.
—Jo-Ellen Balogh
Alpha omega of women: Amy Poehler. —John Evenson
No pride nor prejudice, just passion. (Colin Firth)
—Sherry Ainscough
He makes good girls break bad. (Aaron Paul)
—Sallee Ann Ruibal
Still thirteen when Wahlberg is around. (Donnie Wahlberg)
—Natalie Bath
Move over Joanie, Valerie loves Chachi. (Scott Baio)
—Valerie Reiss

HANNA ROSIN

Start Me Up

I came across an old diary recently. Its first page was a list of questions, perhaps designed to ease the newly minted confessor into the art of revelation: *Name, Age, School, Favorite Color,* and then the last question, *Crush.* It didn't specify "real crush" or "celebrity crush," if that was even a term back then. The first thing that came to my mind when I saw the question was the one game of spin the bottle I'd played in my friend Carl's basement. Did I have a crush on anyone I'd kissed? No, and this was largely my best friend Kim's fault. We lived in an immigrant ghetto in Queens, full of Dominicans, Jamaicans, working-class Jews. But she was German, and beautiful in the exact way the seventies revered—blond, feathered hair, blue eyes. In the sea of mongrels she stood out, a prepubescent Daisy Duke.

I knew it was her the boys really wanted to kiss, so that blocked me from feeling anything for any of them. I was her sidekick, the funny one, the tomboy. When we staged fake weddings at the school playground, I always volunteered to be the usher. She was in the game, but I was still just watching. So on the dotted line in the diary I'd gamely written "Sean Cassidy" (yes, I spelled his name wrong). *Shaun Cassidy.* He of the silky hair and the pinkish lips, always smiling, so sexually unthreatening that in a photo wearing a white cap, he looks like a little girl posing for picture day at tennis camp. I'd seen him singing on TV a few times, a song my mom liked to listen to: "I met her on a Monday and my heart stood still.

Da doo ron ron ron." I saw a magazine with his face on the cover at the pharmacy and spent my ice cream money to buy it. I don't remember feeling exactly swoony, like the girls watching Elvis. It was a crush that in retrospect looks more like a proto-crush, a happy discovery that boys' faces can be smooth and pleasing and pretty as ponies, without the knowledge that sometimes looking at them can feel like getting stabbed in the gut.

Sometime between my tenth and eleventh years I put a big "X" over Shaun Cassidy's name. By that point I had another best friend, Michal, and her house was my refuge. My parents were Israeli and felt like a different generation. Hers were divorced and lived solidly in the seventies, in an apartment building with a pool that operated something like Studio 54. One day Marilyn dyed her hair red and changed her name to Raven. The next day Raven was dating Robert's father, Sam. The next day Sam was holding hands with Jim, and so on. At the pool someone was always playing "I Will Survive" on a boom box. Michal had a much older brother. I couldn't see what he was doing behind the closed door of his room, although occasionally I saw a girl walk out in her underwear. But I could hear it, and in my memory he was listening to the Rolling Stones song "Angie" on an endless loop. One night, I went home from their apartment and in my diary replaced Shaun Cassidy with Mick Jagger.

I don't explain why in the diary but I suspect my new crush also had something to do with getting my period that year, which I did write about. I recalled in the diary that it was an "angry" day. I had gone on a day trip to go horseback riding with a friend's family I didn't know all that well and I had no idea what to do, beyond stuff the toilet paper into my underwear. In my diary I'd also noted that the Boomtown Rats song "I Don't Like Mondays" was playing on the radio on the car ride home. The song still makes me nauseous to this day.

That year I put a poster of Mick Jagger above my bed, a black-and-white showing him in a white T-shirt and a black vinyl jacket, and cocking his head to one side. He, too, looks like a girl; in fact now in that picture he looks to me a little like Lily Tomlin. But at the time I only focused on his lips, which I imagined were saying something like: *Stop hiding. You can come out now.* I bought the album *Goats Head Soup* and started to listen to "Angie" alone, at home. I'd heard the rumor from Michal that in a couple of the verses he said "Andy" instead. How thrilling, how transgressive, that seemed to my soon-to-be-eleven-year-old self, that Mick could love a girl named Angie one day and a boy named Andy the next. What did that mean? Was there a girl in there? And if he could be that shape-shifty then that meant at the very least I could stop being the usher and change places with the one about to be kissed.

To this day, it's the first thing I do when I meet a man: I look for the girl in there, even if she's deeply hidden.

DAVE HOUSLEY

Dynamite

O n the cover of *Dynamite* magazine number eight, Kristy McNichol is smiling the girl-next-door smile to beat all girl-next-door smiles. She looks competent and friendly, approachable and—the word that comes to mind most readily in all things Kristy McNichol—*cute*. If this person arrived at my door right now and asked if we needed somebody to babysit our nine-year-old son, my wife and I would be out the door in minutes. At the time of the photo, January 1978, Kristy McNichol is fifteen years old and at the height of her considerable fame as one of the stars of the television show *Family*. She regularly appears on talk shows and specials, graces magazine covers, and will soon release an album with her brother Jimmy. She is the 1978 version of Taylor Swift, if by the age of sixteen, Taylor Swift had already won an Emmy. She is something we don't have much of anymore, and maybe never had at all, with the exception of Kristy herself: a child star who gracefully delivered on her potential with very little drama. Of course, it is the seventies and we are blissfully unaware of the extent to which our girls next door might soon feel the need to shock us into recognizing that, somewhere along the line, they had turned into women.

It is 1978 and I am eleven years old, a fifth grader at Jackson Penn Elementary School in rural central Pennsylvania. I have never kissed a girl. I am, in fact, terrified of girls, most things having to do with girls, and pretty much everything in the world outside my neighborhood.

To top it all off, I am just beginning to feel the first confusing, terrifying pangs of puberty. It is into this delicate tinderbox that Scholastic Inc. delivers the accelerant of the Kristy McNichol *Dynamite* magazine directly to my fifth-grade classroom. The rest is history, and as they say, history is messy.

It's mostly useless, of course, to try to connect the dots between one's adult life and the things one cared about as a child. My son is fascinated with trains. Does this mean he's destined to be one of those guys, standing by the side of the tracks with a camcorder, or the 2030 version of one, while the Norfolk Southern powers through Altoona?

You know what? Don't answer that.

My first kiss is with Chrissy. She is boyish and slim, with hair that parts in the middle and feathers back over her ears. She is good at soccer and swimming and her father teaches at the same small college where most of our fathers teach.

We are playing a game in my friend's basement. In this game, lights are turned out for designated periods of time. We pair up. We huddle under desks and behind doorways. There is a point to this game, some kind of purported goal, but it is hazy and tertiary at best. Mostly it is the darkness and the pairing and the boyish, cute, athletic girl who will eventually get tired of waiting for me to do something and will, in what is almost certainly an act of exasperation, finally lean over and kiss me.

Before I left for work today, I tweeted, "This morning's totally legitimate writing-related Google search: Kristy McNichol Battle of the Network Stars." That was at seven forty-five. By the time I got to work at eight thirty, four men my age had favorited the tweet, two of them friends from college who I had no idea were even on Twitter. My friend Nick tweeted back a photo of the *Dynamite* magazine cover.

My actual crush on Kristy McNichol is something I carry around with great trepidation, even fear. I tuck it away, cover it up like an embarrassing shirt forced over my head for school picture day. What if my friends knew? My *mother*? It is the seventies and I am eleven and we simply do not speak of such things. Even if I wanted to, I don't have the language for it yet. Crush? More like weakness, defect, character flaw, or "super-weird feeling I get when I look at that *Dynamite* magazine cover."

I don't actively seek out Kristy McNichol. I don't watch *Family*. My contact with magazines that might bear her image is fleeting and accidental, a glance in the grocery store checkout line, a desperate rubberneck into the bedroom of my friend's older sister, a TV ad during *The Six Million Dollar Man* or *SWAT*. And then every now and then I am face-to-face with her image and it's like a quick knock to the head, everything off-kilter and different and hazy and *what is this feeling what is wrong with me is this normal?* It is scary and weird and wonderful for just a moment—that feeling in my gut, in my head, a sweet ache I'll come to know all too well in the coming years. And then I come to my senses and stash the crush away again.

Joan Didion said, "I write entirely to find out what I'm thinking, what I'm looking at, what I see and what it means." When I was presented with this idea—who was your first celebrity crush?—I knew immediately that it was Kristy McNichol. I flashed on the goddamn *Dynamite* magazine cover.

Did the Kristy McNichol cover of *Dynamite* magazine incite my puberty, conjure it out of thin air like a virgin birth? Should I sue

Scholastic Inc. for damages incurred in the following years of desperate moping, for all the time I spent trying to mold my own thickly recalcitrant hair into the perfectly feathered billows on the cover?

The way we consumed pop culture in rural Pennsylvania in 1978 was dramatically different than it is today. We were isolated in a way that I suspect may not exist anymore. If we knew about something, it was because somebody's older sibling told us about it, or we had overheard grown-ups talking, or had scavenged souvenirs of the outside world by picking through old magazines, our parents' books and albums and eight-track tapes. This is how we discover AC/DC and *Carrie,* cigarettes and Boone's Farm and the stack of *Playboy*s that sits, miraculously, in a box in the woods between our neighborhood and the college.

We are like zombies stumbling across the landscape, not truly in control of our faculties, ingesting whatever roams into our immediate vicinity.

This process of discovery, and the absolute nature of those pop culture limitations, is something that will stay with me my entire life. When I find something I love, I still retain that sense of wonder, of fate or kismet or pure, blind luck. With that, there is a grudging restraint, as well, a question of whether this is actually something for me or not. Do I *deserve* to know about this? About Flannery O'Connor or *Kind of Blue* or *The Wire*? Do I really? Me?

A Google image search of "Kristy McNichol *Dynamite* magazine" elicits interesting on-screen results. The cover that moved Fifth-Grade Dave so confusingly, for instance, does not compare well when placed in direct proximity to a similar cover of Valerie Bertinelli. On the cover where Kristy and Leif Garrett lie next to each other like kids taking a break between games of Wiffle ball, they could be twins. She resembles a very cute, very good Little League pitcher. There is no denying it: my first celebrity crush kind of looked like a boy.

In the YouTube video "Battle of the Network Stars Kayak Relay Nov 79 GREG EVIGAN KRISTY MCNICHOL," Kristy McNichol's team of ABC network "stars" battles the Robert Conrad–coached NBC team in an inflatable kayak relay in the Pepperdine University pool. Howard Cosell is doing play-by-play, adding a wonderfully ridiculous undercurrent of gravity to the proceedings. The network stars take this competition seriously, for some reason. Perhaps because the rest of us, watching at home—at least those of us who were eleven years old—were taking it seriously?

What we know is this: "superb athlete" (Cosell's words) Kristy is the anchor, paired against the "excellent athlete" and, as the star of *BJ and the Bear,* fictional truck-driving monkey-partner Greg Evigan. As Cosell waxes dramatic and his partner Billy Crystal interjects tame one-liners, the NBC team takes such a commanding lead that Evigan is nearing the turnaround mark when Kristy hops into her inflatable kayak. For some reason, my forty-eight-year-old self is relieved: she's really good at paddling an inflatable kayak!

There's a moment there, Evigan fumbling with his turn, Kristy moving steadily forward in a businesslike, dare I say LeBron Jamesian fashion (*Superb athlete!*), when I think she just might do it. And that's the thing: even today, as I watch Greg Evigan paddle homeward on my smartphone, a device that would have been inconceivable outside science fiction in 1979, I'm still cheering for Kristy, still thinking there's a chance she'll pull it out.

It is thirty-seven years later and those weird childhood feelings still bubble up like a dormant virus, shingles seeded decades ago by forgotten childhood chicken pox, and the amazing thing isn't how close it makes me feel to Kristy McNichol but how quickly and viscerally I remember what it felt like to be eleven-year-old Dave Housley, sitting in his cool, musty basement with an afghan thrown over his lap, eating popcorn out of a green ceramic bowl and cheering for Kristy to pull it out for good old ABC.

Oh, that kid. He was young and ignorant and isolated. He had terrible hair that never would conform to a McNicholesque feathering. He was scared and safe and innocent and sometimes I still miss him.

NICOLA YOON

Kissing Michael Jackson

kissed Michael Jackson every day for over a year. I kissed him closed-mouthed and open-. When I was feeling chaste, I kissed his nose or forehead or cheekbones instead.

But mostly I didn't feel chaste. Mostly I kissed him on the mouth, full-on. I closed my eyes and pressed my lips to his for at least five seconds. I kissed him so much and so hard that his lips eventually frayed and faded while the rest of his face remained pristine and barely touched.

The way you made me feel, Michael.

I was eight or nine or ten years old when our relationship began. At first I would just say hello, and he would smile his *Thriller* smile and not say anything back.

We (that is to say, I) moved past that shy stage pretty quickly. One morning I woke up and sat staring at him. He was lounging on the ground wearing a black shirt and a suit so white it glowed. A leopard-print handkerchief peeked out of his jacket pocket. It was the smile that did me in, though. He looked like a mysterious angel and it finally occurred to me that I could just kiss him. Who was to stop me? I finally had my own room after a summer spent convincing my mother that my little sister and I needed separate rooms. The guest bedroom was just sitting there unused. I was getting older. I needed privacy. My sister didn't want her own room, but in the preadolescent, selfish way of older sisters, I didn't really care about what she wanted.

The MJ I fell in love with was soft-spoken but not soft. He seemed like he'd be nice to you *and* defend you against all comers. *Just call his name and he'd be there.* He'd be interested in what you had to say. He would hold your hand and call you his PYT. He would ask you how you were and really care about the answer. He would dedicate his songs, albums, and entire concerts to you.

And then there was the dancing. The dancing made me feel things I didn't really understand—a bubbling, fluttering, chaotic, insistent feeling in my belly. The feeling was there even when I wasn't watching him dance. I just had to imagine his face and his I-swear-there-are-stars-in-his-eyes smile. You know: the MJ smile from those days. It was easy and optimistic. His smile said life was good and uncomplicated and so very *fun*. It promised you that you lived in a world that warranted such smiles.

I don't remember when it all began to change for me and for MJ. I don't remember when I went from liking the nice boys to liking the bad ones. It wasn't even about my liking the bad ones. It was just that the real-life flesh-and-blood boys were never as nice as the well-kissed, well-loved poster of MJ that hung in my room for over a year.

Real-life boys were never as nice as the pretend ones in magazines and posters and dance videos. Of course it would eventually turn out that even MJ was not as nice and uncomplicated as he seemed to be.

I remember the brothers across the street from where we lived in the misleadingly named Portobello Heights neighborhood (no mushrooms and just one small hill) of Montego Bay, Jamaica. They wanted my sister and I to pull our shirts up. They were maybe fifteen and seventeen. We were ten and seven. One day, when my mother was still at work and we were home alone, they came over. I don't know what would've happened had their dad not come home unexpectedly early.

My sister and I never let them into the house again.

Still in Jamaica, I remember another boy from school who wanted me to tell him my measurements. My mother found me in the closet with a tape measure and I told her what I was doing. She had two cows instead of the usual one. "He likes me," I told her. That's why he wanted to know my breast size and my waist size and hip size.

Later, in high school in Brooklyn, New York, there was the boy who wanted kisses in exchange for tennis lessons (fair enough). And there was the basketball player who laughed at me in front of all his friends when he figured out that I, a nerdy *and* chubby girl, had dared to be his secret admirer.

Life for the man in the mirror had gone downhill as well. MJ's skin wasn't the same warm brown that it'd been. He was pale. He seemed ill to me. He said it was vitiligo disease. Other people said he didn't want to be black anymore. His cheekbones and nose were suddenly sharp-looking, like you would nick your lips if you kissed them. His hair got longer, and shinier, and flammable. The open smile that I'd loved was now wary and guarded and looked inward instead of out. These were the *Bad* days, the *Dangerous* days.

And there were the rumors. He didn't like women, he liked little boys.

Just before I went to graduate school I met the boy I would lose my virginity to. He was worldly and smart and wealthy, but in the end, he wasn't a great guy. He was hung up on his ex-girlfriend. I really wanted him to love me but he didn't. And in the way of some such relationships, he took advantage of me. He let me love him, and he took what he could get. I do think he was conflicted about it, but he liked it too. He liked being adored. Who doesn't? He liked that I followed him around like a puppy. He liked that I did what he told me. I pined and waited and hoped for his approval.

Until one day. I would like to say now that it was an MJ song that set me free, but it wasn't. I had simply decided to grow up. I decided to love myself over any of the boys, real or imagined.

I decided to go to graduate school and get back to my first love, which was writing.

A lot of people (mostly men) make fun of teenage girls and their crushes. They make fun of the boy bands and the heartthrobs and puppy love. I am not the first person to point out that boy bands and celebrity crushes are not only perfectly natural and harmless, but they're safe spaces for girls to explore their feelings, their physical urges. These crushes are where we form our ideas of relationships and what we want from them and what we can contribute to them.

I spent a year kissing MJ and found that I wanted a boy who was soft-spoken but not soft. A boy who would listen and hear all the things I had to say. A boy who could have me *melting like hot candle wax sensation.*

And when I finally found him, I married him.

PART 2

I Can't Fight This Feeling

Our first celebrity crushes rouse new emotions in us, and those images don't end after the film credits or when we're told to turn off the TV. Sometimes, it's the heartthrob who inspires your sexual awakening. Or it can be the unique individual who brings out the best in you and inspires you to discover—and be—yourself.

ANDREW McCARTHY

The Love Boat

L ove is a powerful elixir. Fame is a potent cocktail. The combination of the two is an intoxicating brew indeed. My own first blush with such heady stuff came of a typically lonely suburban New Jersey Saturday night. Was I fourteen?

Still a few years away from the weekend parties that my older brothers were already attending, parties that would introduce me to drinking and pot and eventually—on a few memorable occasions—make-out sessions, I prowled the house, petting the dog, opening and closing the refrigerator. Maybe I'd listen to music, but never for long. The rich, solitary pleasure of indulgent adolescent musical melancholy was also a few years beyond my grasp. Occasionally I'd talk on the phone with one of my friends, but not often or for very long. What was there to say? Never did I consider reading a book. The scraping boredom of a youth no longer a child but in no way a man percolated inside me like a low-grade fever. Invariably, the TV was turned on.

Reared on the 1970s television "realism" of *The Brady Bunch* and *The Partridge Family,* the likes of Saturday night escapist staples *Fantasy Island* and *The Love Boat* usually did little to engage me. What was there to relate to about an old man in a white suit with a silly accent and his diminutive sidekick, whom I always found disturbing to look at, while they welcomed strangers questing for emotional healing they didn't know they sought, in what was clearly a fake tropical paradise? And nothing about Grover and the gang on that ocean liner filled with folks looking for a second chance at love held my interest. After all, I had yet to have my first fling with love's illusions.

Then one night there she was, walking up the gangplank of that big boat, being greeted by the captain with the long sideburns who used to be on *The Mary Tyler Moore Show*. She had flowing ringlets of shining brown hair, framing an oval face with eyes that sparkled and clearly possessed knowledge of something I didn't.

And there were her breasts—perfectly shaped and straining against the confines of her blouse. All these years later I can't be sure of the color of that blouse—in my memory it is brown—but I know it was cut low. At that point I wasn't familiar with the word "cleavage," but there was cleavage, magnificent cleavage, in all its grandeur. Never in my fourteen years had I beheld such amazing breasts. Had I simply never noticed breasts before? Clearly I had never seen anything remotely like what Adrienne Barbeau was in possession of. What made her even more alluring, and what seemed impossible, was that she appeared oblivious to all this majesty that was hers. This woman seemed frail, wounded. Yet how could someone who possessed such an extraordinary bosom feel in any way less than glorious?

I was mesmerized, bewitched by the paradox of such physical splendor and such emotional vulnerability. As I gazed upon her I ached. I felt sick. Surely, this was love.

I remember nothing of the plot of that episode of *The Love Boat,* although I do have a recollection of poor Adrienne's doelike eyes welling up at one point with an ocean of not-quite-released tears. This only made me want her more. I wanted to protect her. Yet how could I ever protect a woman who possessed such a thrilling bust? It would take more man than I would ever be for a woman with such ample breasts to feel safe and assured. The feeling of impossibility made me want her even more.

Finally I could take no more and I did what any self-respecting fourteen-year-old boy would do. At the second commercial break I ran up to my room and closed the door and masturbated into a sock, with the discovery of the wonder of the female breast—Adrienne Barbeau's breasts—dominating my vision.

Over the years I'd see Adrienne (she is simply Adrienne to me by now) pop up on my television occasionally. I'd always smile. I never felt she was appreciated enough. My love for her had been fleeting but real, educational, and altogether absorbing. If I saw her today, I'd still want to wrap her in my arms to protect her. And perhaps I could.

AMIN AHMAD

The Liril Soap Girl

When I think of my teenage years, of India in the 1970s, the face of the Liril soap girl hangs over it all: her eyes closed, then open, her body shivering slightly, wet with spray. For years she haunted me from the pages of magazines, from giant billboards, from the darkness of movie halls. Even now, many decades later, when I think of her, I feel that slight, sickening twinge of pain. It is because of the girl in the Liril soap advertisement that I have become a connoisseur of the violet ache of heartbreak, the sweeping, sepia-tinted lens of nostalgia.

Let me explain how it happened. Every summer in the 1970s, my mother took my brother, sister, and me to visit my grandmother Dadi in Calcutta. Dadi shared a tiny, two-bedroom flat with my crazy uncle Zia, and our visit involved some radical reallocation of space. My baby sister slept with Dadi, my mother and brother slept in the second bedroom, and Zia and I were relegated to mattresses in the living room. Before he went mad, my uncle Zia had been a newsreader on the radio, and sometimes during the night he would sit bolt upright and bellow, *This is All India Radio. The news, read by Zia Ahmad, on six hundred megahertz . . .*

Needless to say, I didn't get much sleep, and the days were not much better. Dadi cooked all day, and the apartment was full of the smell of frying ginger and garlic. My younger siblings ran through the rooms, yelling and playing their infantile games. At thirteen, I disdained it all and craved some privacy. Taking a book,

I would go outside, sit on the steps of the apartment building, and read. During the day the tenants of the other floors would pass by, smiling vaguely, and say, *Salaam aleikum*. I'd say, *Wa-aleikum as-salaam* back, and keep reading. I didn't give a damn if they thought I was strange; my grandmother was the landlord of the crumbling, three-story building, and I could do as I pleased.

One hot afternoon I heard a rickshaw stop at the front gate, far away down the long driveway. Two figures alighted, an older woman and a girl, and as they walked down the long, dusty drive-way, I couldn't help staring. The girl was as tall as me, with curly, shining black hair down to her shoulders and a heart-shaped face. Her pale skin contrasted with her thick, dark eyebrows and dark eyes, and when she smiled, a dimple appeared in her round, soft cheek. As they passed me, I stood up and clutched the book to my chest and said, *Salaam aleikum,* and the older woman returned my greeting and said, *Oh, so you are here for the summer again? Give my salaams to your mother. You have grown up so much, son.*

But it was her daughter who had grown up. I'd known Sara Khan for years, ever since she was a baby, but something had happened in the year I was away: she had gone from being a brat in a faded dress to a girl with a chest. She was the eldest daughter of a conservative, poor Muslim family and had five siblings. Her father was often late with the rent, and to smooth things over, her mother would sometimes send down dishes of fragrant *biriyani* or *semaye*. I had never paid much attention to this big, messy family who all crowded into a tiny two-bedroom flat, along with their three servants.

Sara and her mother walked past me and went upstairs. Sara did not even look at me, but for the rest of the day I felt restless: the words in my book blurred, and I felt strangely nauseous.

Sara did not come downstairs that day, but the next evening I was sitting on the steps when she walked down with her five siblings, who dispersed all across the long, dusty lawn, yelling and screaming and throwing a ball to one another. Their ayah, an old, wrinkled crone, sat under the mango tree, chewing betel nut and ignoring them all.

Sara was wearing an old, sky-blue *salwar-kameez* with a *dupatta* and looked so grown-up that I was stunned into silence.

She smiled and pointed to my hand.

"Is that a Walkman?" she asked.

I found my voice. "Yes, it's brand-new. One of my father's friends brought it from Dubai."

"I've heard about those. Does it sound good?"

"You want to listen? I've got the new Bee Gees tape."

I put the padded headphones over her ears and pressed play. She closed her eyes and gasped as "Too Much Heaven" flowed into her ears. She opened her eyes at the end of the song and mouthed, *One more song,* and I was happy to comply.

The ice was broken. We talked about the Bee Gees and Donna Summer and Rod Stewart, and Sara said sadly that her mother wouldn't let her listen to this kind of music. It turned out that her life was restricted to school, homework, and evenings spent in their stuffy, crowded apartment.

"So you haven't seen *Saturday Night Fever?*" I asked.

She shook her head mournfully.

"Want me to tell you the story?"

She nodded, and I took a deep breath and launched in on the narrative.

Her ayah was looking at us balefully from under the mango tree, so we walked away, up the long driveway, to the tall iron gate at the end, and back again. I talked and Sara listened, her eyes shining. As it grew darker, her ayah stood, and Sara broke away from me, smiling with regret. She said she would be down the next day.

She was true to her word. This became our routine, walking up and down the driveway each evening, not touching, talking till it grew dark and she had to return to her family. At the end of the first week, I surreptitiously lent her my Walkman and a Donna Summer tape, and when she returned it, taking it out of the waistband of her *salwar,* it was still warm from being pressed against her skin.

How did this romance between us blossom, among all those watching eyes, amid the shouts of her siblings playing with mine, with her ayah watching me like a hawk? Even now, I am not sure.

All I know is that it was late afternoon, and the adults were just waking from their naps and sat bleary-eyed inside, drinking tea. Maybe Sara's ayah was too old and too lazy to intervene. Maybe the fact that I was the landlord's grandson made it permissible; maybe Sara's mother allowed us to walk and talk because it might lead to an advantageous marriage later on. Whatever happened, one of those magic spaces opened up in my regulated world. I lived for those two hours with Sara.

What did two thirteen-year-olds talk about? Those details are lost in time, but we were never at a loss for words. Sometimes we just stopped at the front gate and stared out into the hubbub of the road. There, cars and scooters and three-wheeled auto rickshaws passed, beeping and honking, and we watched the commuters walk by, the men in untucked long-sleeved polyester shirts and carrying briefcases, the women in saris or *salwar*s. We stared at the giant billboard across the road, which advertised the latest lurid Hindi film, often displaying a man with a gun and a bloodstained shirt.

One day we watched as a bamboo scaffolding was erected over the billboard and half-naked coolies swarmed up it, pasting together large, preprinted squares of heavy paper to form the new picture. It took a few days, and we were perplexed by the patchwork of blue and green that was emerging; we could not figure out which new movie would be advertised.

Then, one day, the billboard was complete. There she was, a girl swimming at the bottom of a crashing waterfall, almost obscured by the spray. She was not light-skinned and beautiful like the movie actresses, but brown like us, a normal girl, her eyes shining, her ears sticking out slightly. The tagline showed a bar of marbled green soap and said, *Come alive with Liril freshness.*

We stood stunned, looking at the billboard. It was so devious: only the girl's brown shoulders emerged, and the rest of her was obscured by the crashing water, but it was clear that she was naked. Our minds easily completed the picture. How had they gotten away with this? The government censors watched over nudity closely, snipping out all the sexy bits of foreign films, so that couples moved in for a kiss, and then the film jumped to a chaste aftermath. And it wasn't just Sara and I who were stunned: a crowd of young men had gathered and were gaping up at the billboard.

Sara and I continued on our walks up and down the driveway, but somehow that billboard changed things between us. We walked closer, the soft cotton of her *kameez* pressing against my side, and when I bent my head to hear her better, her curls sometimes brushed against my face, leaving a static shock.

Our talking took on a new urgency. We still discussed music and movies but now we were pushing against something else, the future, looming like the girl on the billboard, just outside the gate. I confessed to her my dreams of going to America, and she said she would like to go, too. She said she wanted to be a teacher and spend her life with little kids.

Looking back, I believe that we—without ever touching, without ever kissing—went through the stages all couples go through: shyness and bravado led to familiarity, to a deepening routine and a shared vocabulary, with our own jokes and references. Our thirteen-year-old selves yearned for each other and found something.

With two weeks left of my visit, I sat on the steps one hot evening, waiting for Sara to come downstairs. I had lent her my Walkman again and waited for her to come down, for us to walk, for her to slip the skin-warmed metal rectangle into my hand. The thought that she had listened to my music, lying in the dark, her eyes closed, made me dizzy.

Sara did not come down that evening. Not the next one, and on the third, her wrinkled ayah limped up to me and wordlessly pressed the Walkman into my hands. I asked her where Sara was, if she was sick, but the ayah just spat out a stream of red betel-nut juice and turned wordlessly away.

What had I done? Walked too close to her? Had Sara been discovered, listening to my Donna Summer tape? Why were we being kept apart?

The deadened days went on, endlessly, and she did not appear. It was then that, overhearing Dadi, I began to piece it together. Sara's father was behind on the rent, six months behind, in fact, and no amount of *biriyani* or *semaye* would alleviate that fact. Dadi had sent Mr. Khan a legal notice, and he had ignored it. Then she had sent my uncle Zia upstairs to talk to him, and there had been words, a loud argument during which my uncle had called Sara's father a "bazaar Muslim."

It was not our fault, after all, but clearly Sara was banned from seeing me. The space that had magically opened closed up again, and no one seemed to notice. Her siblings came down to play every day with mine, her ayah sat under the mango tree and squinted and chewed betel nut. Dadi continued cooking, and Zia went on shouting in his sleep. I was sick with love and maddened at the thought of Sara in the apartment just above me, but no one in my family seemed to notice. I almost went up the stairs and rang the bell and demanded to see Sara, but at the last minute, my nerve always failed me.

The summer ended, and we returned to Madras. Soon I was sent away to boarding school, and my life became very different. That summer in Calcutta seemed like a dream, but though it grew hazy, I could not forget it. Everything was made worse by the fact that the Liril soap campaign was a megahit. Every movie I went to featured the same ad: the Liril girl swimming underwater, emerging by the waterfall, smiling and sleek, bathing joyfully with a bar of lime-green soap.

After school, I went off to America. And Sara Khan? After a long court case, her family was evicted from that flat. They had not paid rent for years. I heard that Sara was "exported," married off abroad, to some Muslim man in Texas. She is probably now middle-aged and fat, like all those women, but in my mind, she is always thirteen and radiant. I tried to find her on the Internet, but I didn't know her married name, and there were too many Saras.

As for the girl in the Liril soap ad, she is perennially youthful and, thanks to the miracle of modern technology, accessible anytime. Whenever I want to, I can log on and see her splash in the waterfall. I can watch her and wait for the violet ache of loss that connects me, across all these years, to a time when India and I were both young, barely awake, and about to plunge into the heartbreak of modern life.

SHANE HARRIS

The Force Is with Mark Hamill

As a five-year-old boy, I harbored an awful secret: I had a crush on Luke Skywalker.

When asked, "Who is your favorite *Star Wars* character?" most of my peers quickly answered, "Han Solo." And why not? He had swagger. He had the *Millennium Falcon*. He was best friends with a wookie.

But Luke, they thought, was lame. And liking him was about as suspicious to the other boys as saying Princess Leia was your fave. The force may have been strong with the budding Jedi, but he whined. About working on the farm. About not being able to go to the academy until next year. He was, it has been said many times, the archetypal callow youth. And to admire him, to want to play him in backyard battles, was to invite ridicule and scorn by boys wielding lightsabers made of sticks. (And to be clear, if you were playing with a lightsaber, you were supposed to be portraying Darth Vader. Being the villain was a more acceptable choice than Luke.)

My brother, six and a half years my elder, manifested his disappointment whenever I cast Luke as the protagonist in my own private *Star Wars* episodes, starring our vast collection of plastic action figures.

Maybe that's why he sold the whole set without asking my permission—to teach me a lesson, or save me from myself. I had always seen past Luke's shortcomings as a protagonist and turned him into the valiant hero, rescuing Chewbacca or C-3PO from near death at the hands of their Imperial tormentors. They may have kissed the budding Jedi to express their gratitude.

Though I hadn't yet conceived of my sexual identity, much less grasped the general concept, I clearly had an instinctive fondness for boys. And Luke was my favorite boy. I was late to the Luke bandwagon (a very short, sad little wagon), having only seen the first *Star Wars* film in the early 1980s, when it was rereleased to coincide with the premiere of the sequel, *The Empire Strikes Back*. I distinctly remember being . . . captivated. I wouldn't have articulated it that way at the time. But I saw Luke on the screen, and I couldn't look away.

I loved his hair. I wondered what he looked like with his shirt off. I wanted to go on adventures with him. My closest real-life analogue was an older boy, a friend of the family, whom I occasionally saw at cookouts or on camping trips. He was about four years older than me, and like Luke, he was tall and clean-cut. I gushed when he paid attention to me. He made me feel grown-up. And I desperately wanted to be taken seriously by people who were older than me.

I thought I was smarter than all the kids my age and that if I stayed too close to them, adults would underestimate me. Whenever my parents had friends over, I gravitated to the grown-ups, engaging them in what I suppose I thought passed for enlightened conversation. I remember pulling out my Speak & Spell and trying to impress my parents' friends with all the nouns I knew.

I steered away from kids. Truthfully, I was afraid of them. I was terrified of being teased for my preferences—I was into not just Luke but teddy bears, and had a massive collection—and being asked to participate in sports, for which I had no natural aptitude. But even at five, I was a natural conversationalist, and this delighted adults to no end. Nothing made me prouder than to hear a grown-up exclaim to my mother or father, "He's so mature!"

Looking back, Luke must have seemed to inhabit a magical space right between childhood and adulthood. He was a grown boy.

Not a man. My infatuation with him wasn't confined to the realm of fantasy and my imagination. I knew that he was a fictional character, and I was also drawn to the real person who played him in the movies: Mark Hamill.

Now, let's be honest. To have professed a crush on Mark Hamill—at any age—would have inspired more confusion than derision. If there were any fellow Luke lovers among my friends in suburban Portland, Oregon, they weren't coming out. He was never a leading man, even when he *was* a leading man in a major Hollywood franchise.

His post–*Star Wars* film credits attest that casting agents weren't persuaded of his star power. Hamill followed up his turn as Luke Skywalker with unmemorable roles in *The Big Red One* and *The Night the Lights Went Out in Georgia,* starring Dennis Quaid and Kristy McNichol.

Unlike most film producers, I wanted to know as much about Mark Hamill and his acting potential as possible. I actually read movie posters whenever I was at the theater hoping to find another Hamill movie. I watched behind-the-scenes stories about the making of the films, eager for any scrap of biographical material. I bought *Star Wars* books on audiocassette with a read-along pamphlet. I probably should have consulted *People* or movie magazines to learn more about Hamill's backstory, but my research never progressed beyond ancillary marketing materials—which is kind of hilarious since I ended up becoming a journalist. What a missed opportunity this was to learn about the profession.

The only major press I remember Hamill getting after shooting the first *Star Wars* movie—and it was unavoidable because it was all over TV—was that he was in a horrible car accident that left him disfigured, so for the sequel, Luke was mauled by a snowman to explain why he looked beat-up.

I worried about Mark. When I saw Luke in *The Empire Strikes Back* hooked up to tubes while a robot nurse tended his wounds, I imagined that's what Mark must have looked like in his real hospital room, damaged, vulnerable, and fighting for life. I was also very pleased to see that the filmmakers had shot the scene with Luke in his underwear! It felt like I was seeing something I really shouldn't, but it must have been okay, because why would they put it in the movie? Let's say this was my first time being titillated.

This was around the time when it dawned on me that my fondness for other boys extended beyond friendship or star worship. I remember at age six learning the word "homosexual," when I heard it in *Stripes,* which came out in 1981, the year after *Empire,* in the scene where Bill Murray and Harold Ramis are being interviewed for the army. (Apparently, much of my early social education was thanks to the movies. I also learned about alcoholics by watching *Arthur.*)

I was watching the movie at home, and a friend of my brother pulled me aside and told me that homosexuals were men who liked other men, and that the label was undesirable and to be avoided. He was a handsome boy, too, like the friend of the family I idolized. But he was also reckless and constantly getting into trouble. I was wary of him, but he had street smarts, so I believed what he said. Gays were bad. Looking back, I'm convinced he was one.

If loving Luke Skywalker as a fan was contemptible, loving him as a man was apparently dangerous. I honestly can't say whether I began to realize at that moment that when kids had teased me for liking Luke they were actually insinuating that I was in love with him. But after being told that gay was bad, I don't remember wanting to learn any more about Mark Hamill's biography or his acting career.

I harbored the secret that I was gay until I was twenty-two. That was plenty of time to develop more crushes on actors, and to learn the difference between infatuation and yearning. But the fear of ridicule was strong with me.

That first crush was also a first lesson: that one's opinions and preferences can be so distasteful to others that they're actually threatening. It took me until my early twenties to say that I'm gay because I was convinced that once the world knew, avenues of opportunity would be closed off to me. The adults who were delighted with my five-year-old precociousness, who just *knew* I was destined for big things, would learn my secret and think, *Oh, what a shame.*

So I kept quiet, which sometimes is the path of least resistance toward self-preservation.

I think that a good number of my childhood friends must have also thought Luke was their favorite character, but they'd have never admitted it. And I don't think they liked him because they were gay, but just because Luke was more a boy than a man, and at such a young age, we'd naturally identify with him more than Han Solo. Really, he was for the older boys. And the girls.

When I finally came out, it was a relief beyond anything I'd ever experienced to honestly tell people who I am and what I want. If I look back now and put the physical attraction to Luke Skywalker aside, my crush obviously revealed more about my personality than my sexuality. I saw myself in him. I, too, thought adults didn't see what I was capable of achieving. I also felt separate from my peers and was propelled by a need to outshine them. And like Mark, I had an instinct to perform and to become someone memorable.

That instinctive sense that Mark and I had something in common must have been why, at age five, I began investigating Mark's backstory—to find out how he became a successful person (even if his acting career didn't take off at light speed).

My crushes today tend to be defined more by admiration for people's achievements than physical attraction. Mostly they're on writers, many of them decidedly not famous, and a handful of actors. Maybe a painter or two. Very few celebrities can make me weak in the knees.

But my crush on Luke abides. It is one of the most tangible sensations of my childhood. And it was my first feeling of wanting to know someone deeply whom I'd only seen from afar. That force will be with me. Always.

JASON DIAMOND

The Secretary

One day when I'm old, and a bunch of kids gather around me to ask what life was like in the 1980s, I'll say that I recall it being a time when everybody wanted an actor to be president, everybody wanted to wear the suit with the biggest shoulders, and everybody wanted to rule the world. It was the decade when everybody wanted a lead role. I'd also remind them that I was really too young to develop any real philosophical thoughts on the age as it was happening, that my first few years of life were shaped by the 1980s, but that I'm caught in that weird gray area where I can claim dual citizenship as part of Generations X and Y; that I liked the big stars, but it was the decade's greatest supporting actress that I liked even more.

I was four years old the first time I saw Annie Potts on film. I remember it so clearly, sitting in that quaint single-screen movie theater, the kind that is pretty much all but extinct in this age of massive Cineplexes. I was seeing *Ghostbusters* with a babysitter, acquainting myself with my new heroes, Bill Murray and Harold Ramis, and bracing for the parts that would scare me; after all, the word "ghost" was in the title. But besides the two early scenes that revolve around a specter haunting the basement of the New York Public Library, I'd gotten myself worked up over nothing.

That is, until I beheld the secretary, with her big glasses, short hair, and nasally voice. Even at my young age I could tell she was obviously attracted to Egon, the Ghostbuster I most associated with, thanks to his glasses and Semitic features that reminded me of just about every adult male in my life up until that point. You only see her a few times throughout the film, but every time you do, she's showing off a different side of the character: she can hang with the smartass Peter Venkman, she is interested in reading and playing racquetball, and when things seem the most dire toward the end of the movie, she's supportive and sweet to Ramis's Egon Spengler. Her star shone brighter even than the movie's special effects, considered cutting-edge in 1984.

When you're that young, attraction is not what it is in adulthood, or even adolescence; things like love and heartbreak, surprise boners, awkward first dates, good first dates with people you never hear from again, and unexpectedly running into an ex with their really great-looking new significant other are things you can't contemplate. All you have is feeling. You see somebody and you know that there's something different about that person; you can't quite put your finger on it, but it's there. It's not love, it isn't sex; it was a feeling, and that's what Annie Potts was to me. When she came on the screen for the first time, everything slowed down; illuminated in my little-kid mind with a kind of glow I wanted but couldn't quite make sense of. Words often fail children, as they see and experience far more than they can process verbally. Phenomena are reduced to single words with a heart-stopping immediacy exclusive to the very young and new. Why was I feeling this thing I couldn't describe?

A few years later, I was a second grader who had finally moved on from thinking girls were gross. I'd gone through what I understand is a common developmental quirk: repulsion because I didn't understand attraction. I had a girlfriend now, a girlfriend named Alana Meyerwitz who kissed me on the cheek under the monkey bars at recess, signed notes that she flipped to me during class with "I love you," and told our mutual friends that we were getting married one day. I just went along with all of it. I wasn't exactly a young Casanova, but I was slightly more interested in girls than, say, multiplication and division, and a few of them feigned interest in me, especially Alana. Instead of claiming they had cooties, I now found girls mysterious and cool.

Nineteen eighty-seven was still pretty much peak Molly Ringwald. She was coming off three very successful John Hughes films that helped redefine the teen movie, and to top it off, *Time* magazine had featured her on a May 1986 cover, an honor that, back then, was one of the highest any cultural figure could receive. So when another babysitter came to my house to watch me on a Saturday with a freshly released VHS tape of *Pretty in Pink,* I recognized the young ingénue despite not having seen any of her movies. In my mind, Ringwald sat alongside Michael Jackson, Madonna, and Michael Jordan as the most important cultural figures on the planet. And yes, I thought Ringwald was pretty, but it felt more like it was my duty, like every American had to memorize her roles just like we had to be able to sing along to "Thriller." I felt pressured to see at least one film starring the redheaded teen actress, especially since—supposedly—all of my friends had seen everything she was in and were very familiar with the work of the rest of the Brat Pack, the cadre of young actors and actresses she hung out with. I was not yet ushered into the group of kids who could quote from her other movies, left on the sidelines of their conversations. Sure, I could laugh at their jokes, but I was far from a featured player on the playgrounds of my youth. I wanted to be included, and to do that, I had to somehow familiarize myself with Ringwald's oeuvre. So we watched.

Yes, I loved *Pretty in Pink.* Ringwald as Andie was pretty and cool, making her own clothes, driving around in her vintage car, and not showing that she gave a damn about what the cool kids thought. I envied Duckie's sense of style, and even James Spader as Steff, the pretentious preppy bad guy who looked and acted a lot like the kids who picked on me for being brainy and Jewish. He was an asshole, sure, but he looked so great doing it. I saw something I liked in almost all of the characters in the movie, but one in particular really caught my attention: Iona, Andie's eccentric boss at the record store.

She was older than Andie, Duckie, and the rest of the high school students; we don't get to hear too much of Iona's backstory. *Pretty in Pink* is a movie about teens, so the all-grown-up Iona is rightfully at the perimeter of the action. What we do get is a new style from the character in every scene she steals, from hair spiked straight up like she's on her way to a Siouxsie and the Banshees concert, to a groovy beehive, to a straight technofuturistic bob bleached impossibly white. Iona is the cool adult—she wears heavy eye makeup, latex, and even fluffy yellow slippers just because she wants to—but what's more important is that next to the sweet and innocent Andie, there's something wild about Iona. She is an enigma, to us and to Ringwald's wide-eyed protagonist. Even as a kid, I picked up on that distinct strangeness—and I liked it.

I found Iona *attractive,* or at the very least—once again—I felt something I couldn't explain. It feels almost gross to say that seven-year-old me found her sexy, but that's really the only way to explain it. I was already hooked, but during one of her scenes in the record store (the one where she dons a red snood in the style of 1940s noir) it all came together for me: her slight Southern accent fell away to reveal the woman who played Janine, the Ghostbusters' secretary. Janine was playing Iona. Iona was Janine! Iona was Janine was Annie Potts! My synapses, firing simultaneously and in all directions, eventually calmed, leaving one fact in the wake of my discovery: I had a crush on Annie Potts, and any time I saw her name in the credits, which was quite a bit in the 1980s, I paid attention.

But the thing I noticed was that while Annie Potts's name frequently popped up in movies, she was never the star. A part in Whoopi Goldberg's *Jumpin' Jack Flash,* another appearance as Janine in the second *Ghostbusters,* and the sultry and evil villain opposite John Candy's bumbling, good-guy private detective in 1989's *Who's*

Harry Crumb? Of course, Potts had plenty of success in the 1980s and into the '90s on the popular television show *Designing Women,* but the truly wonderful leading movie role she sorely deserved ended up escaping her.

Yet none of that mattered to me. Annie Potts didn't need to be the star for me to like her. Her status as sixth or seventh in the credits, never at the top of a poster or mentioned in the previews, affirmed my notion that she was a very rare talent indeed, glimpsed only for a moment now and then. I connected with her because she seemed real compared to her colleagues. Because even though she wasn't in as many scenes as the stars, the ones she was in were the ones I paid the most attention to. She was the perpetual supporting actress of my younger years, but no leading lady could ever compare with Annie Potts.

PART 3

We Belong Together

We imagine our best selves in our celebrity crush's eyes. Because we spend so much time with them, we feel like they really know us—deeply—and we them. We feel destined to be best friends and soul mates, yet alas, there's not much chance that we'll ever meet the crush who's occupying this precious real estate in our heads and hearts. But that doesn't stop us from holding out hope.

ROXANE GAY

The Decent Man

Whenever I am asked about my favorite books, I inevitably mention the *Little House on the Prairie* books by Laura Ingalls Wilder. As a child, I read these books with devotion and obsession. They were so full of vivid descriptions of settler life. Oh, how I wanted to make candy with maple syrup and snow. Laura, aka Half Pint, was bright and willful and charming. These books showed me that it was possible to tell stories about being a girl from the Midwest, like I was, and have those stories matter.

And then, of course, there was Almanzo "Manly" Wilder. If I have a first love, it is that man of good Midwestern stock. I loved him because he was always steady, true, handsome, courageous, strong. He tamed wild horses. He was a hard worker. He was good in a crisis. He loved fiercely, deeply, and knew how to be romantic in subtle, unexpected ways.

Some of my most indelible memories from the *Little House on the Prairie* books involved Almanzo. There was the time he won a buggy race even though he had his horses pulling a heavy wagon. There was that time he and Cap Garland braved brutal winter weather to bring wheat to town so the townsfolk wouldn't starve. That Almanzo was such a mighty good man.

My favorite moments with Almanzo were in *These Happy Golden Years,* where Almanzo and Laura's courtship flourished. In the book, Laura is teaching during another frigid winter, far from home and all alone. Almanzo comes to the rescue each weekend, with his amazing horses and a cutter. He makes sure Laura is warm and gets to see her family. Even though she is kind of salty toward him, Almanzo continues showing up each week. After her teaching contract is over, Almanzo picks Laura up in town and takes her on sleigh rides. When spring comes, he takes Laura on buggy rides. He lets Laura drive and admires how she can handle boisterous horses. When Nellie Oleson tries to weasel her way into Almanzo's affections and Laura tells him he has to choose, he makes the right choice.

There's more. After he proposes and Laura accepts his hand in marriage, Laura asks Almanzo if he wants her to promise to obey him. (I also had a crush on Laura, who knew how to stand up for herself and was never going to give her entire self over to a man just because she fell in love.) Almanzo, my beloved Almanzo, he says the perfect thing. He says, "Of course not. I know it is in the wedding ceremony, but it is only something that women say. I never knew one that did it, nor any decent man that wanted her to." When he said those words, some part of me was betrothed to Almanzo forever. I am always going to be very fond of a decent man who knows when to tame something wild and when to let it run free.

MICHELLE BRAFMAN

Harry Chapin: A Crush of the Soul

Harry Chapin came into my life when my brother went off to college and unwittingly gave me carte blanche over his record collection and stereo. It was 1980, and I was sixteen. I found Harry's *Greatest Stories Live* nestled between Marshall Tucker's *Carolina Dreams* and Bob Dylan's *Blood on the Tracks* and spent long hours lying on my back on my brother's red shag carpet, absorbing ballads about the broken dreams of dry cleaners and waitresses and taxicab drivers.

My crush on Harry was atypical. It was not romantic in nature. He was ancient: in his late thirties, practically my parents' age. My crush was one of the soul, because I felt as though he'd peered into mine. His story songs were full of longing and thwarted dreams and love between ordinary, sometimes homely, people. If the "broad who served the whiskey" in "A Better Place to Be" could find love with the midnight watchman, I could hope. I had friends I adored, but I never went to a high school dance or had a boyfriend. As a swimmer, I was taller and broader-shouldered than the boys in my class and felt as awkward as the waitress who wished that she were beautiful enough to snare her lonely patron.

I used my leftover bat mitzvah money to acquire *Verities & Balderdash* and *Portrait Gallery* and cash from odd jobs to purchase Harry's entire oeuvre and peppered my private motivational talks with lines from his songs. "For every dream that took me high, there's been a dream that's passed me by," I'd tell myself after losing a swim race or enduring rejection from a real love interest.

A few months into the crush, a wondrous thing happened. Harry Chapin was coming to the Milwaukee Performing Arts Center, and my father knew the promoter. I was going to get to meet "the gardener and weed puller of my inner landscape," a term appropriated from one of Harry's album liner notes.

I was so thrilled about the concert that I told everyone I knew, including my brother's friend Dave, who wasn't starting college until winter. It turned out Dave was more than hip to the B sides of Harry's records, and that was enough for me to reconsider this perfectly pleasant boy whom I'd written off as one of my brother's meatheaded friends. If Harry understood me, and Dave understood Harry, then I'd found a soul mate by proxy.

I invited Dave to the concert. I wore a blazer and plaid wool skirt, memorialized in a photo that I've turned my basement inside out to find. I could barely breathe when I spotted Harry talking to a group of middle-aged donors at the pre-concert reception to raise money for a world hunger organization. I memorized every detail of his appearance, although it wasn't his looks that I loved. He had frizzy brown hair like mine and a square dimpled chin, and he wore a madras shirt. I recognized his booming Brooklyn baritone with a dollop of smartass and the sadness that bubbled beneath the crust of his charisma. The promoter introduced us. I said something stupid, and he kissed my cheek.

Throughout the concert, while I sat between Dave and my parents, I kept touching that cheek. Harry sang right to my tortured late-adolescent soul, and when he did his shtick about asking the audience to respond to alternate endings to his song about a banana-truck mishap, I bellowed along with the rest of the auditorium, "Harry, it sucks." I didn't understand it then, but this was either more than or less than a real crush, because what else is a crush but a repository for our own passions and unfulfilled real-life relationships?

Harry was connecting me to Dave and the hundreds of fans who were hollering along with me. Despite my sanctified cheek, it wasn't Harry I wanted; it was his ability to make me feel a part of his choir of lonely voices.

My fixation with Harry deepened my bond to my brother as well. When Lester came home from college that spring, we memorized the entire fourteen minutes of Harry's autobiographical song "There Only Was One Choice," punching the lines that mattered to us. Now I had a way to distinguish between the "I like 'Cat's in the Cradle'" fans and the diehards who knew the lyrics to his opus, including the prescient line "I fantasized some tragedy'd be soon curtailing me."

That summer, I met the biggest Harry diehard at a high school program at Yale University. The first night I walked through the hall to the dining commons, Chris was playing "A Better Place to Be" on a grand piano. He was skinny, with greasy hair that parted in the middle, and he spit a little when he said the words "paper bag." But never mind all that. We spent hours together, him singing, me listening and requesting more songs. We made a plan to see Harry in concert, but we never made it.

A few weeks before the show, a tractor trailer on the Long Island Expressway hit Harry's Volkswagen from behind. Harry died.

I was inconsolable. My friend Katie said that she'd been through the same thing only months earlier when John Lennon had been shot, but I knew it wasn't the same. Only Chris understood my loss. After the summer ended, however, we never saw each other again. The only thing we had in common had been our mutual enjoyment of Chris's performing Harry's songs.

Harry's songs not only guided me toward these odd and fleeting kinships but they planted seeds deep in my subconscious, and his appeal to my adolescent angsty self grew into a passion for stories. I learned that Harry was right, that "the capturing of whispers" was the way to make a sound. I became a documentary producer and fell in love with the kind of dirty realism and heart I'd found in Harry's stories.

As I grew into adulthood, my musical tastes shifted toward female vocalists like Joni Mitchell and Shawn Colvin, but I wanted to tell Harry's story so badly that I ended up producing a segment on him for VH1's *Behind the Music* and began working on a documentary film. A friend introduced me to Harry's stepsister, who, in turn, introduced me to his widow, Sandy Chapin.

In the summer of 1996, Sandy invited me to stay at the home she'd shared with Harry and their family and we had dinner at a Mexican restaurant in Huntington, Long Island. We talked about Harry's social activism, and I took a piece of that conversation with me as a reminder that you can make art and be in service of a larger idea, yet if you thought about that cause while you were actually making that art, it could turn out really horribly. Afterward, I lay in Harry Chapin's guest room, once occupied by his youngest child, his "Dancin' Boy." I had a premonition that I would never produce this film. And perhaps in the spirit of a crush, I was more attached to the idea of Harry and the power of his stories and social conscience than I was to the idea of rooting around in the lives of the people he'd left behind. I never produced the film.

I continue to find more die-hard fans because I look for them: a psychic in San Diego, a cousin, a traveling companion on an airplane, a mom of one of my son's friends. Last winter, my husband drove my family to Syracuse from Washington, DC, to bury my sister-in-law. We were all exhausted after her long brutal death, each in our own world, feeling alone and a part of our family at the same time. I picked up my iPhone and sent out a message in a kind of Morse code to my Facebook world. "We're approaching the hills that lead into Scranton, Pennsylvania," an obscure line from "30,000 Pounds of Bananas." I closed my eyes while we traveled through the snowy hills, my phone in my hand, humming with every new response to my call to known and unknown Harry fans, to the compassion that he drew out of us all.

JESSICA ANYA BLAU

I Gave Birth to Tatum O'Neal

The fantasy went like this: Tatum and I (both around ten years old) are on the beach in Malibu, walking along the wet sand, hand in hand. A moving wall of a wave roars toward us and we run from it, still holding hands, our bodies perfectly aligned with each step. Later, as the sun sets, when the ocean fog pads in and the temperature drops fifteen degrees in fifteen minutes, we huddle together, our backs to the cliffs and our butts scooted into the sand. We face the water and watch the oil rigs light up like ocean-wading dinosaurs wearing Christmas lights. Our bare legs are cold and goose-pimpled so we pull our big T-shirts over our knees, making it look like we have giant jutting breasts (a bosom like that of my great-grandmother Bubbe, who spoke to me in incomprehensible and spitty Yiddish).

This was the kind of stuff I already did with my friends on the beaches about eighty miles north of Malibu where I grew up. But after the first time I saw the movie *Paper Moon,* I wanted to do these things with the movie's star: Tatum O'Neal.

She was pretty as anything: straight, dirty-blond, corn-silk hair; wide-set blue eyes; a creamy round face. In the movie she smoked cigarettes, ran a con game, and wore a beautiful cap with a thick lace band that encircled it like a garter around a thigh. After the fifth time I saw the movie, my mother bought me a hat like that—or as close as you could get to a hat like that. I wore it to school every day for a couple weeks, ignoring the boys who teased me and explaining to the girls, "It's like Tatum O'Neal's hat in *Paper Moon*." Sometimes, after school when my friends and I were riding bikes, or climbing the lemon trees in the orchard that backed against my house, or walking up and down the chalk-white sidewalks on stilts (taller than a grown-up and utterly unafraid of the falls that invariably came), I would think about how Tatum would fit in perfectly. She'd love stilts. She'd love the smell of the lemon orchard. She could probably roller-skate just as fast as me. And the ceiling game? The one where we took mirrors off the walls, held them (glass-up) under our chins, and then walked around the house staring into the mirror and pretending we were walking on the uncluttered cottage-cheese-looking ceilings—I'd have bet Tatum would love that, too. But the beating heart of my fantasy, what I really wanted, was to live in Malibu next door to Tatum and to be her best friend.

I didn't tell anyone I had a crush on Tatum O'Neal. It never came to me in those terms. I had crushes on boys and on my teacher—a surfer who once got in a fistfight with one of the Beach Boys. But what could you call my moony thoughts about Tatum other than a crush? She entered my mind when I lay in bed at night; or sat alone at the dining room table where I'd been left behind, instructed not to leave the table until I'd eaten *three bites of meat;* or when my father took me to the hardware store, where he could wander for a couple hours, just looking at things, amazed at all the possible creations that could come of wood, bolts, and screws. I read everything I could about her in magazines and the newspaper, and I made my chatty family shut up when Charles Bronson and Jill Ireland read off the Academy Award nominees for Best Supporting Actress that year. When Tatum won, we all screamed and then everyone hugged me as if she really were my best friend.

I suffered my greatest moment of childhood pride the Thanksgiving following the Academy Awards when, gathered in the living room at our family friends' house, Lila (one of my mother's pals, who wore a Rolling Stones T-shirt with an image of the giant lips with the tongue licking out) said to me, "You know, you sort of look like that girl, that little actress girl . . ." She pointed at me, thinking, searching for a name. *Tatum?* I wondered. *Could she possibly be talking about Tatum?* I was, and am, brown-haired and brown-eyed. I was covered in freckles. I didn't think I looked anything like Tatum. Naomi, our hostess, asked her, "What little girl?" Lila hemmed and hawed and spoke her way around it, the way grown-ups often do: "That cute little blond girl, the one who was in that funny movie, what was that movie?" *Paper Moon,* I thought. But, stunned, I sat there in my normal silence and waited to see if she was really working toward the one thing I wanted her to say.

"Do you mean that *Paper Moon* movie?" Naomi asked.

"Yeah, the one with that little girl who won the Academy Award."

"What are you talking about?" My mother had wandered into the room with an unlit cigarette in her hand. She sat on the hand-hewn coffee table and then lit the cigarette using the pack of matches that sat next to the glass ashtray stuffed with lipstick-stained butts.

"Jessie," Lila said. "She looks like that little girl from that movie *Paper Moon.*"

"Tatum O'Neal," my mom said. She inhaled deeply on her cigarette and then blew out a stream of smoke before leaning into me on the couch and kissing my cheek. "Jessie loves Tatum, don't you?"

"Yeah," I said, blushing, and then I rushed out of the room, shimmering with the thrill of having been connected to Tatum by people outside of my own brain.

A couple years later when I hit puberty and became boy crazy, the Tatum fantasies were replaced by images, ideas, and scenarios far more complex and tantalizing. I didn't think of Tatum often, but I still made it to her next movie, *The Bad News Bears,* on opening day. Over the following decades the Tatum press was slim, but my mother made sure to let me know whenever she read something about her in the paper. Her marriage to John McEnroe, in particular, intrigued me. Tennis was the only sport I'd ever watched in my life (the only sport that was ever on TV in my house). In short, he was one of the few athletes I actually knew by name and, oddly, someone I had a crush on.

Following the O'Neal-McEnroe nuptials, I watched Mac's matches with additional interest as I waited for the camera to land on Tatum in the stands. She usually looked glamorous, half-bored, smiling and clapping appropriately when her husband played well. I went to the French Open once but was unable to bribe my way into the McEnroe match (as I did the Lendl one) and never spied Tatum in the stands. Then, around 1991, I went to the Canadian Open. John was playing a doubles match, although he was mostly retired then. It's not a big tournament and the stadium isn't huge, and when I wandered off and was semi-lost trying to find something to drink, I found myself suddenly halted by security. John McEnroe was coming out of a locker room surrounded by a team of men. He stared intently into my eyes as he walked toward me. We remained visually locked until he had passed. I was starstruck, of course, but my mind didn't follow the normal flow. These were my first two thoughts: 1) *As with Lila, decades ago, do I remind him of Tatum?* And, 2) *Is Tatum here?*

Shortly after that encounter, I gave birth to my first daughter, Maddie, and my brain instantly shut off from the world outside of motherhood and writing. I missed all of *Seinfeld* and *Friends* in their first run, rarely flipped through a magazine, and probably never thought of, or about, Tatum O'Neal.

My second daughter, Ella, was born in 1996. As with her sister, I immediately loved Ella in that half-loony deeper-than-infinity way. But, somehow, I was not infected with the maternal blindness that makes you think that just because it came out of your body, it's beautiful. At birth, she was decidedly *not* beautiful: a puffy-eyed, bald old man, the color of a spoiled pomegranate. Every week, though, Ella got prettier and prettier. And then, when she was school-aged, I was staring at her one day and I gasped. Ella was the spitting image of Tatum O'Neal. Same corn-silk hair, same slightly Asian blue eyes. Big, wide smile. I called my mother and told her, "Mom, I think I gave birth to Tatum O'Neal."

Ella's physical and sartorial progression has mirrored that of the young Ms. O'Neal: Tatum with bangs, check! Tatum in overalls, check! Awkward brown-haired Tatum at puberty, check! Tatum with long blond hair, a summer tan, and a flashbulb smile, check, check, check! And because Tatum's childhood personality— her love of the beach and her readiness to roller-skate or play any kind of game—was a creation of my imagination, Ella has been Tatum's equal here, too.

One day this past winter, my family was hanging out on the beach in Santa Barbara. Maddie was sitting on a rock reading, Ella and I were picking through a tide pool, and my husband, David, fiddled with the slo-mo feature on his newest iPhone. David asked Ella and me to run toward the camera. I grabbed Ella's hands and she dug her heels into the sand. I tugged her arms like someone pulling the reins on a stubborn mule. "Come on," I said. "Let's just do it." She said she was cold. I said it would only be a minute. She said it was embarrassing. I said no one was watching. She said she was tired. I said the run would wake her up. She said okay, she'd do it, but only once. David walked far away from us so he could get the shot as we came toward him. "Ready!" he yelled. Ella and I clasped hands and we took off, our knees lifting in unison, our feet hitting the sand at the exact same moment. We ran and ran and ran—precisely in sync—parallel sides of the same machine. It was a spectacular moment. A perfect moment. My Tatum-and-Jessica-on-the-beach fantasy come true. Only better.

by
♥ JANICE "SOLDIER OF LOVE" SHAPIRO ♥

CRUSHABLE

"JOHN LENNON"

OKAY!

YOU GUYS WANT TO SEE SOMETHING?

MY SISTER, EVELYN, AGE 8

ME, AGE 7

SUSAN DUFFY, AGE 10

1963
LATE ONE AFTERNOON, OUR NEIGHBOR FROM ACROSS THE STREET CAME OVER. SUSAN DUFFY WAS TEN, THREE YEARS OLDER THAN ME AND TWO YEARS OLDER THAN EVELYN. SHE WAS TOO OLD TO PLAY WITH US, BUT TOO YOUNG TO BABYSIT. USUALLY WE DIDN'T HAVE MUCH TO DO WITH HER.

WHY ARE THEY CALLED THE BEATLES?

I DON'T KNOW.

ARE THEY NICE?

FIRST IN AMERICA COMPLETE BEATLES STORY
ALL ABOUT THE BEATLES
"THIS IS OUR LIFE" BY THE BEATLES THEMSELVES
A WEEK WITH THE BEATLES

I DON'T KNOW.

SUSAN HAD THIS MAGAZINE ABOUT THIS NEW MUSICAL GROUP FROM ENGLAND CALLED THE BEATLES.

I DON'T THINK THE OTHER GIRLS' AVERSION WAS SOLELY BECAUSE JOHN WAS MARRIED AND WORE GLASSES.

PERHAPS IT WAS BECAUSE AS HARD AS THEY TRIED TO MASK JOHN'S DARK/MEAN/ACERBIC PERSONALITY IT COULDN'T BE COMPLETELY SUPPRESSED.

HIS SMILE WAS REALLY MORE OF A SMIRK.

HIS EYES REFUSED TO BEG FOR ADORATION.

THERE WAS NOTHING CUDDLY ABOUT JOHN.

SO, WHY WAS I ATTRACTED TO HIM?

ME THINKING ABOUT IT NOW

DID I REALIZE THAT HE WAS THE TRUE LEADER OF THE GROUP? PERHAPS THE SMARTEST OF THE FOUR?

WAS MY ATTRACTION TO JOHN A RECOGNITION OF A FELLOW PRODUCT OF AN UNHAPPY FAMILY?

JOHN WAS THE ONLY BEATLE WHO WAS NOT RAISED IN A TWO-PARENT HOUSEHOLD – ACTUALLY HE WAS BROUGHT UP BY AN AUNT.

COULD I HAVE SENSED "SOMETHING CRIPPLED" INSIDE HIM? THE SAME THING THAT WAS BECOMING CRIPPLED INSIDE ME WITH MY DISTANT FATHER, MOTHER WITH UNPREDICTABLE MOODS AND AN OLDER SISTER DETERMINED TO DESTROY MY SELF-WORTH.

"...CAN'T HIDE WHEN YOU'RE CRIPPLED INSIDE..." *

* A POST-BEATLES' JOHN LENNON CONFESSIONAL SONG.

JOHN LENNON WAS TOUGH, AND SINCE I DID NOT FEEL PARTICULARLY SAFE IN MY CRAZY FAMILY, COULD I HAVE IMAGINED JOHN AS A PROTECTOR?

IF YOU WERE MY BOYFRIEND, MY SISTER WOULD BE TOO SCARED TO EVER BE MEAN TO ME, JOHN.

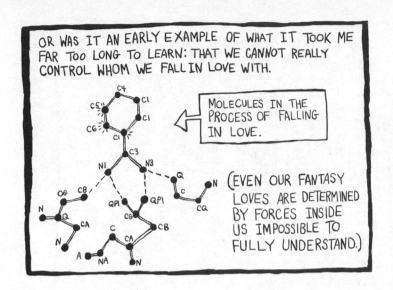

WELL, TIME PASSED....

...AND AFTER THE BEATLES BROKE UP, THERE WAS A MAJOR SHIFT IN THE WAY PEOPLE VIEWED THE WORLD. STARTING AROUND 1971, JOHN SUDDENLY BECAME EVERYONE'S FAVORITE BEATLE.

♪ NA NA NA NA ♫

JOHN LENNON IS MY IDOL, MAN. HEY, DON'T BOGART THAT, AGAIN!

PAUL IS SUCH A WIMP!

EVERYONE KNOWS JOHN WROTE ALL THE GOOD SONGS.

I KNEW IT! I KNEW IT! I KNEW IT!

OH, GOD, I'M SO HIGH. WHAT DID I KNOW, AGAIN?

AS I GOT OLDER, MY NEED FOR MASS ACCEPTANCE LESSENED.

I DON'T NEED EVERYBODY IN THE WORLD TO LOVE ME ANYMORE, JUST EVERY COOL PERSON IN THE WORLD.

AND ACTUALLY, ONCE EVERYONE LOVED JOHN LENNON, MY INTEREST LESSENED.

MY TEENAGE BEDROOM FLOOR

HONESTLY, I LISTENED TO "IMAGINE" ABOUT AS MUCH AS I LISTENED TO "RAM," PAUL McCARTNEY'S SOLO ALBUM—WHICH WAS APPROXIMATELY NEVER!

I DID CONTINUE TO BE ATTRACTED TO THE REBEL TYPE. (OTHER CRUSHES I HAD DURING THAT TIME)

PEAK YEARS OF CRUSH 1970-1972 ULTIMATE HIPPIE LONER.

NEIL YOUNG

1972-1975 THE GREAT SEXUAL REBEL (TRUTHFULLY, HE TERRIFIED ME, BUT I LOVED HIS MUSIC)

DAVID BOWIE

1977-(WELL, FOREVER) LEADER OF THE L.A. PUNK BAND, X, AND WHAT IS MORE REBELLIOUS THAN A PUNK?

JOHN DOE

PART 4

I Want to Be You

A crush isn't always the object of your romantic affection. And yet, these unattainable celebs inspire us in actionable ways throughout our lives. Sometimes it's the person who triggered a passion deep inside you that led you to your career. Or it's the young man or woman who symbolized everything you wanted to become. You've heard of the bromance; well, this is the prequel.

JAMES FRANCO

Crushin' on River

I saw *Stand by Me* at my uncle Michael's house in Shaker Heights, Ohio, when I was about twelve, the age of the boys in the film. Michael now has two grown boys of his own, but then he didn't. After the film, after we heard in the last Richard Dreyfuss narration (a technique of an adult in VO telling about his younger self—the younger self played by Wil Wheaton—that *The Wonder Years* would capitalize on) about how River Phoenix's character, Chris Chambers, pulled his life together, and became a lawyer, only to be killed prematurely when breaking up a knife fight in a McDonald's, Michael said, "I've never had friends like I did when I was that age [twelve]." In some ways this is true for many people; it is a time of innocence and exploration, on the cusp of adulthood, which is very much what the movie was about: four boys going on an adventure into the wilderness to see a dead body, and along the way they entertain themselves by singing the pop songs of the day (1950s) and discussing the pop icons: who would win in a fight, Superman or Mighty Mouse, and the growing size of the Mouseketeer Annette Funicello's breasts, which pretty much encapsulates the first blush with the wider world that *is* puberty. The movie captures this time of life so well, and was so instantly nostalgic (it was made in the '80s but set in the '50s, the way *Freaks and Geeks* was made in the 2000s about the 1980s), that it will always be a touchstone for coming of age.

But for me, I think something else was going on. I was not only drawn to the characters in the movie, I was drawn to the actors, especially River, playing the young little bruiser with a heart, who had an ineffable quality so that despite playing the character known for being the bad boy in school, and not the raconteur stand-in for Stephen King, who could tell entertaining stories about Wide Load barfing at the pie-eating contest, he came off as much wiser and knowing. I wanted River's character, Chris Chambers, to be *my* friend; actually, I wanted *River* to be my friend. But even more than that, I wanted to *be* River. I wanted to be an actor, and I wanted to act like *him*. And after reading River's biography, and Corey Feldman's recent autobiography, *Coreyography,* I saw that when they made that movie about coming of age was when those boys actually came of age. I wanted to have my own personal development be recorded on film; I wanted *in*. But it seemed like a club, something out in Hollywood that I, living in Northern California, would never be a part of. For me, River *was* acting, and I was in love.

When I was in high school I became obsessed with Gus Van Sant's movie *My Own Private Idaho,* and especially with River in that film. River rewrote the campfire scene where he tells Keanu's character that he loves him. It is his best performance. He died two years after it was released.

Later, after I worked with Gus on *Milk,* he allowed me to edit my own version of *My Own Private Idaho* because he had saved the editor's reels. I did a version that focused on River's character, Mike Waters. I ended it when Mike is strung out on the street, partly because that's where River died, on the sidewalk of Sunset Boulevard, outside the Viper Room, the night before Halloween.

Later I became a professional actor, but River was long gone. I wrote him this poem because he still means so much to me. I don't know if he would have liked me if he knew me, but he has been my idol as an actor, from before I was an actor to now. A young angel who guided me when I was young, and guides me still.

RIVER

Hello, James, it's River.
Where do you think I'm calling from?
Deep in hell, deep in the Florida
wilderness?
Deep in the cement bowels of LA,
Beneath the neon, and the signs?

It's me, River, calling you
From the underworld.
I died at age 23,
Ten years before your age now.
James, you're the Jesus age.

You think you know me?
I tried to be something good,
Something that spoke to people,
I was pushed into acting, but I loved
music,
You're in acting because you chose it.

Pick up the phone, James, it's River,
I'm calling to say it's over.
You know that moony feeling,
Like the air is gone, because there is no
More of a life? I've left just a little,

I know you want more, James,
But I left only a little.

And what time
Do we have for others
Anyway?

I've been gone for decades,
I've been forgotten.
I spent my two decades
Focused
On work and family.

You're all over the place, James.
I was a River that flowed straight
And pure; you're like a king
That orders one thing,
And then orders the opposite thing.

JOANNA RAKOFF

Little House

One warm Monday afternoon, a week or two before my eighth birthday, my friend Heidi came up with a plan: On Friday, after school, rather than roller-skating or drawing or making ramen in her microwave, we would take a walk. A long walk. A walk that constituted an adventure, an expedition, a journey. We would hike from our quiet, tree-lined, winding street—Tamarack Lane, main artery of the Redwoods, a subdivision of modern California-style houses, all cathedral ceilings and steeply angled windows—to the nearest place in which one could conduct any sort of business: a small, newly built strip mall, consisting of a Grand Union, a pharmacy owned by one of our neighbors, a pizza parlor, a dry cleaner's, a Baskin-Robbins, and a craft shop that sold the sort of things eight-year-old girls in the 1980s desired more than anything else, like three-dimensional satin unicorns and Lucite boxes custom-painted with rainbows, ribbons for weaving into the grooves of steel barrettes, and rhinestones one could embed in T-shirts after one had cut the necks off. Heidi and I—and our friends Jodi and Zinnia, Brie and Susan, countless Melissas and Jessicas and Jennifers—could not get enough of this store. We could spend hours, days, poring over the different shades of rhinestones available, the curve of a satin unicorn's haunch. Our mothers, not surprisingly, could barely stand to be dragged into it, much less convinced to purchase anything. Sometimes, at night, after I'd turned off my flashlight and set down my book, I calmed myself to sleep—I had been having trouble sleeping—by thinking about this shop, or about the ways in which my life would change were I to somehow obtain something from it, even the tiniest satin rainbow.

But this plan, Heidi's plan, had less to do with this magical place, or even the tantalizing aisles of the pharmacy, filled, as they were, with *Betty and Veronica* comics, issues of *Mad* magazine, and every type of candy imaginable. Heidi's plan—and I knew this implicitly, before she offered a word of explanation—had only to do with the thrill of the journey itself. Because, you see, as I said, this was the 1980s. The 1980s in the suburbs. Pomona, like most true suburbs, aggressively lacked sidewalks. We did not walk anywhere. We could not walk anywhere. Or, rather, within our immediate neighborhood we had free rein; we could run over to each other's houses—no advance phone call required—or ride our bikes up and down the silent streets, or play hopscotch near the curb.

Over the days that followed, we plotted our journey with Magellan-worthy intensity: to the end of Tamarack Lane; down the steep slope of Chestnut Drive; right on Quaker Road, the wooded country thoroughfare on which stood remnants of Pomona's past, crumbling colonial-era houses and ramshackle Victorians; and out, finally, onto Route 202, the main thoroughfare, on which sat the little strip mall. We knew this route as well as we knew our own minds, for our mothers drove it every day, once, twice, three, four times, as often as we needed milk or calamine lotion or our father's shirts from the cleaners. And yet walking this path—with its mere three turns—struck us as a truly grand adventure. All week we talked of nothing else. At night, as I struggled to sleep, I fantasized about our walk, equal parts apoplectic with excitement and terrified. I could imagine Heidi and I walking to the end of our street—that part I could see—but my mind simply couldn't picture us going any farther. Never, in all my years, had I seen anyone—much less two third-grade girls—walking on the side of the road. Was this even allowed? Would we be arrested?

As it happened, my family had moved to this particular town, Pomona, from a river hamlet twenty minutes south, Nyack, where one could in fact walk everywhere. My older sister told stories of walking to school, to the shops downtown, to the park, which I repeated to Heidi—and Jodi, Zinnia, the Melissas and Jennifers—in hushed tones, as if describing Oz or Narnia or Xanadu. A place where kids could walk to the store and buy a pack of Twizzlers! Just like the towns and neighborhoods in the books I read: *All-of-a-Kind Family, Anne of Green Gables,* Beverly Cleary's Ramona novels. Books in which kids ran free and had adventures—collecting trash from the dump, adopting stray dogs, floating down rivers—largely unfettered by parental involvement. I wanted, in a raw and desperate way, such a life.

Though perhaps more than anything, I wanted one specific life: the life of Laura Ingalls Wilder. Not—and it's painful for me to admit this—the Laura Ingalls Wilder of the *Little House* books. Oddly, though I'd plowed through nearly everything else in the children's section of the local library—from Lamb's Shakespeare to Judy Blume—I'd not read them, primarily because my mother had told me, over and over again, that they were "boring." But, rather, Laura as portrayed by Melissa Gilbert on the television show adapted from those books, a show that, if you were a child in the 1970s and 1980s, perhaps you loved as fervently and obsessively as did I. Perhaps you, too, spent hours wandering through thin suburban rafts of trees, imagining yourself Laura, on the prairie, catching frogs and befriending raccoons. Perhaps you, too, attempted to smooth your wild hair into shiny braids, while the girls around you spent hours with a blow-dryer, flipping their hair into Farrah Fawcett waves. And perhaps you, too, were bookish, like Laura—perhaps you remember, as I do, the scene in which she studies while making dinner, a book propped by her mixing bowl.

Perhaps you, too, wanted to be as kind as Laura, to be the sort of person who befriended the new girl with the limp and defended the kid everyone else mocked.

And perhaps you, too, loved Laura because she was the only character on television that in any way resembled you, because she didn't, like every other girl character on television, fall roughly into a type—the pretty-but-shallow girl, the tomboy, the fat girl, the wise-ass. Laura was simply Laura, idiosyncratic and complex. She loved to play in the mud and read books. She loved her doll and kicking a ball. She loved and respected her teacher and her parents but didn't hesitate to speak out if she thought them wrong or misguided.

Nor did she hesitate to show anyone how she felt. In fact, she seemed incapable of hiding her anger or sadness or joy—a skill I was told, by my mother, I needed to better master—and yet the world seemed to respect, to love her more, for it. There is a moment—a horrible, wonderful moment—in the first season, the Ingalls' second year on the prairie, when Laura confesses to her father that she's responsible for her little brother's death—though she's not, of course—then collapses in huge, great, soul-quaking sobs. Her father, Charles, holds her and begins to sob himself, the family's vast, overwhelming grief—for this baby, dead after only a few days of life—finally overcoming him. I had a brother and sister who had died, too, as children, a year or so before my birth. Their portraits, in pastels, hung just across the room from where I sat, in what my mother called the "family room," which held the television and our board games and books. I had just learned of their existence, these ghost siblings, and it did not escape me that I would not be sitting on the couch, watching reruns of *Little House on the Prairie,* if they had lived, which was something akin to causing their deaths, though I did not know the actual cause of their deaths. And that afternoon, I sobbed along with Laura and Charles, engulfed by the force of their emotion, muffling my tears in the polyester blanket we stashed for cold nights, its cover imprinted to mimic a patchwork quilt—the sort, actually, that adorned Laura and her sister Mary's attic beds, but lacking, of course, in such an item's texture or history.

If you're thinking, perhaps, I had a sort of girl crush on Laura Ingalls Wilder, I suppose you would be correct, though it was only for a time. Once I'd smoothed my hair into those braids, I begged my mother for smocked dresses and long skirts and high-necked blouses. In the depths of summer and in a certain light, my decidedly brown hair looked a bit auburn, and I wondered if I could get away with calling it "reddish brown." When a few freckles appeared on my nose, I rejoiced.

But it would, in some ways, be just as accurate to say that I had a crush on Laura's world. A world, yes, where kids could roam free, and could take on the sorts of responsibilities—moral and domestic—relegated, in my day, purely to adults. A world in which children were respected and more was expected of them. But, most important, a world in which someone like Laura could be loved and appreciated for herself, thorns and all. For me, each day felt like a struggle to contain my unwieldy thoughts and emotions, to tuck myself away so the bullies wouldn't pounce and my mother wouldn't grow angry or frustrated with me. "You're so sensitive" was perhaps the phrase I heard most often as a child. In Laura's world, it was good to be sensitive, to be honest, to be kind. In my world, it seemed more important to be tough and impermeable. "I can stand anything other than crying," my mother would often say when I burst into tears. "Stop crying right this instant." Which made me long, of course, to bury my head in my mother's lap and cry more, as Laura did.

Because perhaps I had a crush on Laura's mother, too, in her infinite kindness and forgiveness. And certainly I had a crush on Charles, who always, always had time to play with his daughters and also time to involve them in his work, but who also had time for everyone who needed him, who lived his life according to an inner set of ethics that seemed lacking in my own brash, suburban universe, a universe in which everyone seemed intent on proving how little they cared about anything, anyone at all. "Ask me if I care" was the most popular retort among the kids at my school, and even some of the teachers. On *Little House,* Charles cared about everyone, about everything. He cared unquestioningly, he cared because caring was, for him, part and parcel of being human. Which was how it struck me, too. My existence, so often, felt like a restraining wall, against which a tidal wave rushed. What had changed in the world? When had we all forced ourselves to stop caring? To prize cool over warm?

But that year, the year I turned eight, something happened: Laura met Almanzo Wilder. And, in essence, fell in love with him at first sight. As, it seems, did I. Perhaps you remember the scene? In a fog of love, she mangles his name into "Manly," then runs away, embarrassed, sure that he thinks her a stupid kid. Decades later, I can recall every instant of that scene, down to the brilliant sunlight shining in Laura's eyes as she looks up at him.

Not long before that episode aired, a photo appeared on my friend Zinnia's otherwise bare bedroom wall: a close-up of a smiling man with hard blue eyes and curtains of feathered hair falling to either side of his cheekbones. He looked vaguely familiar. "Who is that?" I asked. Zinnia rolled her eyes. "Parker Stevenson," she said. "From *The Hardy Boys.* Everyone likes Shaun Cassidy. But I think Parker is cuter." I nodded. "They're both cute," I said, though I wasn't entirely sure who they were. A few minutes later, I explained that I had to be home for dinner. Out on Tamarack Lane, I walked home slowly, pausing over the detritus of suburban life: a small snake crushed by a car, which my friends and I had been watching decompose, with horror and fascination, for a good week; a crowd of ants devouring someone's lost cheese curl; the flowers that fell from various peach trees. I'd found the man in the photo repulsive, the opposite of "cute," with his overly styled hair and egotistical smile. So repulsive that I'd fled Zinnia's room, shaken by the image—the idea that she truly found him cute—but also shaken by the fact that Zinnia, my quiet friend, whose parents were as strict and old-fashioned as my own, found *any* boy, or man, cute. Cute enough to hang his photo on her wall. To widen her eyes when she spoke of him. I was baffled.

And then Almanzo appeared on the screen in our family room. And I suppose my eyes widened in that same way. When Laura looks up at him, overwhelmed with emotion—for he radiates a goodness, a kind of inner brilliance that makes the world fall away—something unleashed deep in my chest, sliding down to my stomach. He was ten years older than her—twenty-five to her fifteen—on the show as in real life, and part of her instant adoration has to do with the fact that he's a fully formed human being, a man, like her radiant father, rather than a boy, pounding sticks into the dirt and pulling her braids. He has put away childish things. Except, perhaps, kindness.

Our grand adventure was never to be. "Your mom," I asked Heidi, the Thursday before we were due to set out, "is okay with this?" She nodded solemnly. Her mother was a film producer—as was her father—and rarely present in Heidi's immaculate, elegant house. Instead, a series of housekeepers presided over Heidi and her vast collection of dolls. I had only glimpsed her mother once or twice, at Heidi's elaborate birthday parties. "It's not a big deal," Heidi said. "It's just a walk." She gave me a hard look. She knew my mother. "You don't have to tell your mom. She'll never know." Was this true? I wasn't sure. What if my mom, thinking I was at Heidi's, drove by us on Route 202? Or, more important, what if something happened to us on the way?

The next day, when my mother asked what my plans were for the afternoon, I told her about our walk. "I think that's a little too far," she said. "I'd be happy to drive you." We didn't want to drive, I explained. The whole point was to walk. My mother looked at me uncomprehendingly, as if I'd suggested a trip to the moon or a ride in a submarine. "But if you want to go to the store, why not just drive?" she asked. I shrugged, unsure of how to answer. What would Laura say? I wasn't sure. Would she have gone anyway? Probably. "I promised Heidi I'd go," I told my mother, stupidly. The tears were already gathering at the back of my throat. Why couldn't my mother understand? Why couldn't I find the words to explain? Of course, the minute I'd uttered our plans aloud, the idiocy, the hollowness, the futility and pointlessness of them became all too clear. "I'll call her and tell her I can't go," I said, my throat thick with tears. Tears for what? I wasn't sure.

The next week, I turned eight; Heidi's gift: a satin unicorn, its hindquarters lightly brushed with blue, like a cloud. Heidi hadn't taken our walk alone, as she told me she would on the phone that day; her housekeeper had prohibited her. But as recompense, she'd driven Heidi to the craft shop to buy my birthday gift. I hung it by my window, from the nylon thread knotted to its back, and at night, as I struggled to fall asleep, gazed at its shadow on my pink-flowered walls. I had, over that year, as I struggled to sleep, come to almost love the night, the shifting of my eyelet curtains, the murmur of my parents from the family room, the cool, calm dark, in which I could be purely alone, a closed book on my nightstand, emitting rays of promise. But now, more and more, I thought of Laura, in that blinding sunlight, gazing up into the more brilliant sun that was Almanzo, and so drifted off into sleep, for a day when I might be so warmed seemed, somehow, possible, even if it was a far way off, many journeys and adventures away.

KERMIT MOYER

Me Tarzan

My infatuation with Edgar Rice Burroughs's Tarzan of the Apes started in the summer of 1955 when I was not quite twelve years old and my family was living on the island of Okinawa, where my mother, my sister, and I had come on a military troop ship to meet my army-officer father, who had come by plane from Korea, where he had spent the past fourteen months. In the preceding year, while my father was away, my sister had managed to lose most of what we called her baby fat, and I had earned a string of straight A's in school, doing so well, in fact, that my sixth-grade teacher had told my mother that, if we liked, I could be promoted directly to the ninth grade and skip junior high school altogether. But it was an opportunity my father had vetoed as soon as my mother wrote him about it. "He would feel like a freak," my father had written back. "He would be three years younger than everyone else in his class." But to acknowledge my academic success, he gave me a book that he thought might appeal to me and that he said might also be something of a challenge since it was clearly intended for adult readers rather than for an eleven-year-old boy. Apparently the first volume in a series, the book was entitled— rather thrillingly, I thought—*Tarzan of the Apes*. The author had three names, Edgar Rice Burroughs; the book's copyright date was 1912; and although I could see from the first words that reading its verbose nineteenth-century prose wasn't going to be easy, I was sure that with a dictionary and a little effort, I'd be able to make my way through it. I very quickly discovered that, if anything, the pleasure of reading was only heightened by the concentration that reading such old-fashioned language required.

Tarzan's African jungle was located on the farthest periphery of the known world—exotic, primitive, and distant—which was one of the things that most attracted me to the book, since that was much the way I regarded Okinawa. There may not have been any great apes or lions or gorillas in the grassy fields and woods of the island, but danger lurked nevertheless. There were unexploded hand grenades and land mines left over from what had been one of the bloodiest battles of World War II, live ammunition that, if we came across it, we were warned not to even think about touching. We were also told to be on the lookout for the deadly habu, a venomous snake native to the island that was said to be related to the king cobra. I carried a pocket snakebite kit to supply first aid just in case I got bit by one of them whenever I went out "reconnoitering," as I called my explorations of the surrounding woods and the abandoned cavelike tombs that had mostly been bulldozed to make way for the suburban-style concrete houses with lawns and sidewalks where the dependents of American army, air force, and marine officers and en-listed men lived. There was no television on Okinawa, and although we occasionally went to a movie on the base, reading became my chief form of diversion. And imagining myself as Tarzan of the Apes became more than a diversion—it became a refuge and even provided me with what you could call an alternative form of identity.

Whatever its stylistic excesses, Burroughs's language succeeded in conjuring up for me a hero who embodied everything that I could have wished I might someday become. But the farther into the book—and then into the series of books—I read, the more I began to realize that, even if this heroic version of myself that I yearned to become could only ever exist in my imagination, that might be enough.

Tarzan was described as having a "straight and perfect figure, muscled as the best of the ancient Roman gladiators must have been muscled, and yet with the soft and sinuous curves of a Greek god," a physique in which "enormous strength wondrously combined with suppleness and speed." And Tarzan's inner qualities—his intelligence and his innate sense of justice—were just as significant as his good looks, his physical prowess, and his muscular strength: "With the noble poise of his handsome head upon those broad shoulders, and the fire of life and intelligence in those fine, clear eyes, he might readily have typified some demigod of a wild and warlike bygone people of this ancient forest."

There was also the animal keenness of his senses (my senses, too, at least for as long as I could imagine I was inside his skin). Having such acute senses meant that wherever Tarzan might be, he was intensely *there*. His olfactory nerves were as sensitive as a bloodhound's. Burroughs pointed out that because human beings depended largely on their ability to reason, they had let their senses atrophy—but not Tarzan. From early infancy, his survival had depended upon the acuity of his perceptions, so his senses had become preternaturally acute, whereas except when I was inside a story, I was so nearsighted that I sometimes had trouble reading the blackboard at school, and I absolutely refused to wear glasses—after all, would Tarzan ever have worn glasses?

Tarzan's intelligence was such that it enabled him to teach himself to read English, even though, at the point when he learned to read it, he had never even heard it spoken. Superior intelligence was something I was also beginning to pride myself on, and an innate sense of justice was something that I was sure I possessed, too, because I was never in doubt about what was fair and just and what wasn't, although I realized in later years how blind I had been at the ages of eleven and twelve to the racism and class bias in Burroughs's treatment of Tarzan's hereditary gifts. When Tarzan meets Jane Porter, the woman who will become the love of his life, he treats her intuitively with "the grace and dignity of utter consciousness of self. It was the hallmark of his aristocratic birth, the natural outcropping of many generations of fine breeding, an hereditary instinct of graciousness which a lifetime of uncouth and savage training and environment could not eradicate."

It turned out that, like me, Tarzan had two identities: if he was Tarzan of the Apes, he was also John Clayton, Lord Greystoke, and he was defined as much by his aristocratic blood as he was by his feral upbringing and his savage environment. One of my favorite fantasies was that, unbeknownst to everyone around me, I, too, was actually a foundling prince, and that the couple who were raising me were no more my real parents than Kala, the female ape who adopted the infant Lord Greystoke, was Tarzan's true mother. Kala had raised Tarzan to be as strong and as self-reliant as he would have to be to survive in the jungle, given his lack of claws and fangs and his pale and furless skin. His name meant White-Skin—a feature that in the jungle put him at a distinct disadvantage. It was thrilling to imagine such complete isolation and vulnerability, and then to watch as this "ugly duckling" turned into a swan to beat all swans. *Tarzan of the Apes* felt like a scenario for my own ugly-duckling transformation.

I was also struck by the similarity between Tarzan's displacement to the African jungle, where he had been left, alien and alone, both an exile and an orphan, and my displacement to what was called the Far East, where I too felt like an exile and a stranger.

When I discovered there was a volume entitled *The Son of Tarzan,* it made me wonder what it might be like to have Tarzan for your father. My father had promised to read that volume with me, but although we knew the book existed, we were never able to locate a copy, so I had to imagine what it might be like on my own. What complicated the fantasy for me was the fact that it was on Okinawa that my father's drinking became a serious problem. He'd always enjoyed a cocktail or two, but now it got to the point where he was going to bed drunk nearly every night, and Tarzan's virtues—especially his extraordinary self-discipline and the sober rationality of his intelligence—couldn't help but stand out in bold relief against my father's slurred words and sappy grin and flushed face. Alcohol seemed to dissolve his native intelligence and make him stupid and sentimental and somehow defenseless. My mother tolerated it, I think, only because it never got so bad that he couldn't function—and, besides, she sometimes liked to join the party herself. So on a Sunday evening, my sister would crayon or play with her doll collection, my mother and father would sit on the patio and smoke cigarettes and get drunk with their friends, and I would be wherever Tarzan was in the book I was reading.

The next day, reading *Jungle Tales of Tarzan* on the school bus, I would chuckle to myself thinking of what would happen if Tarzan were actually to step onto my school bus one day—none of these other military kids would know what to make of him, any more than they knew what to make of me. In contrast to the boring familiarity of the suburban world we lived in, even on Okinawa—a world where it felt like everything was known and repeated ad infinitum—Tarzan's African jungle world was filled with surprise and savage intensity and a hard-edged consequentiality that I both hungered for and feared. My life was just the opposite. It was like the contents of my brown paper lunch bag, which I knew without having to look—ordinary, unappetizing, and predictable—like my father's daily hangovers. Moving to Okinawa hadn't really improved anything. We seemed to bring a trivializing everydayness with us wherever we went. Only in books could I hope to escape it.

Because the truth was that only the imagined world of storytelling felt real to me. It was the only world where everything fit together and made sense, the only place that seemed commensurate to my sense of life's promise. Compared to my interior identity as Tarzan, my public identity seemed as unsubstantiated and as insubstantial as a rumor, hazy and formless, full of inchoate longing and a sense of vague disappointment. My alternative identity as "Tarzan" might only be available to me through the evocative power of words, but it was reliably there, and as long as I could read and my imagination worked, I could enter that interior world whenever I wanted to. My identification ran so deep, in fact, that it would come as a shock to see my public self by accident in a mirror or reflected in a window.

The charm of Tarzan's jungle world lay precisely in its darkness and its eruptions of savagery so fierce and deadly that they made the problems of my home life seem entirely negligible. Tarzan was an irresistible combination of primal instinct, muscular strength, brains, and an elite aristocratic lineage, but what I identified with most of all, I think, was his outsider's sense of being both wounded and challenged by the fact that he was in a kind of exile from his true home. But where was that exactly? It certainly wasn't Lord Greystoke's England, because Tarzan didn't even set foot on English soil until he was well into adulthood. But it wasn't the African jungle either, any more than Okinawa was my true home. My true home, I had begun to discover, was nowhere but inside my own head, and in the same way, I reasoned, although the printed pages of a book might have been Tarzan's place of birth, his true home was also inside my own head. Not where he came from but where he ended up—and where he still remains.

The Chosen

Our father died during the summer of 1988, and half a year later, absent his steady guiding hand, it seemed that our family—from my mother on down to my little brother—was in a state of rebellion.

Only a few weeks earlier, my mother had switched from the floral kerchief she'd worn for a decade and a half—the mark of the exceedingly pious—to the more common headgear for Brooklyn's Hasidic women: an elegantly styled wig. My little brother, Mendy, at nine, began to insist on wearing high-top sneakers, even though his school considered them "goyish," a vulgar American fashion. My elder sister, Chani, and I, though our relational status ordinarily swung between heated animus and chilly indifference, colluded on the most rebellious act of all: watching movies.

It was she who came up with the idea. "We can rent a VCR," she said. "My friend Miri can get us movies."

I knew nothing about VCRs, or movies, except that they were sources of profanity and corrosive to the spiritual health of a Hasidic boy. My sister, however, at sixteen, was worldlier than I, and she had even worldlier friends. She knew a place that rented movie-watching equipment by the hour. Her friend Miri, known on our block as a *prusteh meidel* for her short skirts and for chatting with boys, had a membership at the video store at the edge of our neighborhood—the same video store that, for years, my father and I would pass on our way to shul on the Sabbath, and he would place his hand over my eyes when they wandered to the posters in the window.

But our father was dead, and our mother didn't care, and there wasn't much else to do besides.

It was during the intermediate days of Passover. I was fourteen, studying at a Montreal yeshiva, but now home for the holidays in our Hasidic community of Borough Park, Brooklyn. Ordinarily, I spent my days from six in the morning until ten at night immersed in sacred texts, with the occasional break for a dunk in the ritual bath, a prayer service or two, and the odd meal. All of that was now suspended, though, and without the structure and routine of the yeshiva curriculum, I felt fidgety and restless.

Passover is an eight-day holiday, but only the first and last two days are wholly sacred, on which there are extra prayers and festive meals and special foods and endless rituals to keep the days flowing. The four intermediate days are only semisacred: special enough to take off from weekday routines, to keep kids home from school and adults off from work, but otherwise involve lots of sitting around with little to do.

Part of me wished for the lesser tedium of the study hall. I had already read every book in our home, scoured every drawer for something to hold my attention—an old Rubik's Cube; a set of *kugelech,* the Israeli jacks my friends and I used to play with for hours on end—but all those old childhood diversions no longer satisfied. The feeling of boredom was overwhelming, and it was hard not to consider the forbidden. And so my sister's movie-watching suggestion sounded like just the thing.

Several hours later, on the floor of my sister's bedroom, lay the television set and VCR box, and beside it, a pile of rented videocassettes.

There was an air of freedom in our apartment, and transgression. Movies and television were forbidden in our community, as were radio and newspapers. All secular influences were suspect, and I now felt an unusual mixture of excitement and apprehension.

My sister had other ideas, though. As it turned out, the dozen or so dramas and romantic comedies she rented were mostly for herself. She allowed me to watch selected parts of *Ferris Bueller's Day Off* (shooing me out when sparks of teenage romance struck—"You're too young for this") and only one other movie, which she rented especially for me and which she left me to watch on my own: *The Chosen.*

Despite having little to compare it to, I realized quickly that *The Chosen* was an unusual film. In one of the first scenes, a line of teenage Hasidic boys ambles into a Brooklyn schoolyard, and I had a startling realization about the world. Until then, I had known that the outside world did not know us, did not understand us, and we did not understand them; so it had always been, so it always would be. But now, here on this television set, on this *profane vessel,* I saw my world reflected back to me—a 1940s version, to be sure, but close enough. And within this reflected world, within that line of boys, was a boy after my own heart: Danny Saunders. Earnest, softspoken, with a beaver hat and coat that could've come from my own closet, with sidelocks curled as perfectly as my own. Danny loved his world, his people, his traditions, but he also had a rebellious side; he hungered for knowledge, for experiences, for encounters with the outside world.

The film, based on Chaim Potok's novel by the same name, is a story of friendship between two boys, Danny and Reuven, and it is also a story of fathers. Danny and his father, Reb Saunders, are Hasidic. Reuven and his father, Mr. Malter, are not. It is his father that Danny loves and respects, and to whom his heart belongs, but his mind belongs to the modern world of Reuven and Mr. Malter.

Hungry for intellectual stimulation, Danny visits the public library in secret—oh, how I envied him in those moments!

Throughout my childhood in Borough Park, I had so often passed the public library on Seventeenth Avenue and Sixtieth Street, right at the periphery of our Hasidic enclave, but I never thought to enter it. It was like a rule of nature: rain is wet, the moon glows round in the night, and public libraries are not for Hasidim. But I did look for books in musty corners of variety shops along the edges of our neighborhood, in the homes of more worldly neighbors, and, on occasion, in my sister's bedroom. I knew Danny's desire to step across the boundaries.

Danny, however, had a special interest, one I knew little about. "Deep inside of us," Danny tells Reuven excitedly, "there's something called the unconscious! It makes us do and feel things without us ever being aware of it!"

"How do you know all this?" Reuven asks, and Danny, shyly, confesses about his secret library visits.

"It's okay with *me*," Reuven says with a shrug.

"But not with my father," Danny says. "He's very specific about the things I read."

Danny, however, doesn't let this affect his enthusiasm. He has been reading about psychology, and he can barely get the words out fast enough: "Adler! Jung! Freud! It's incredible, Reuven! It's exciting!"

Still, he knows, he will not be able to fully immerse himself in the subject that animates him so. His future has already been written—his destiny is to remain a Hasid, to follow in his father's footsteps and to spend his life dedicated primarily to religious studies. Reuven will go off to college, but for Danny, rabbinical yeshiva is the only option.

Unless. Unless something comes along, as happens in movies though rarely in real life, and Danny's father comes around, allows his son to continue studying his modern ideas, to learn more about the unconscious, and the symbols in our dreams, and our unknown desires. A boy, even a Hasidic boy, can dream the impossible, and it might come true, as it does indeed, in the end, for Danny.

I watched *The Chosen* once, then rewound the tape and watched it again, and then again. It was only with difficulty that I tore myself away, as the last two days of the holiday approached, and the rented equipment and the videocassettes had to be returned. But the movie itself left me dreamy, unsettled, with a painful yearning to be not only watching that movie but to be *in* it.

This, I would realize later, was my primary relationship to Danny: I envied him. I envied his experiences: his first visit to a movie theater, his non-Hasidic friends, the dream-come-true ending to his story. But even more, I envied him for his story being told.

In the days following, I walked through the streets of Borough Park and saw myself as if in a film, a film like *The Chosen,* with me as the central character. My character, too, had secret dreams. My character, too, wondered what mysteries the world held and whether I might access them one day. My character, too, had a story! Didn't I deserve a movie, too?

I imagined eyes. Eyes everywhere, observing my every step, every twist of my shoulder, every sideward glance. Walking to shul each morning, I acted the part of a boy who went to shul each morning. Coming home, I acted the part of coming home. My world, which had once been real, was now pretend. Instead of a Hasidic boy in Brooklyn, I was an actor playing a Hasidic boy in Brooklyn—and what a boy he was! Handsome and thoughtful and intelligent with a darkly mysterious side because he was so much older and wiser than his years, because he had *lived* so much—all the self-indulgent narcissism of adolescence finding expression in my *acting,* playing a character within a world I saw as fully artificial even as it was fully real.

"Robby Benson is *soooo* good-looking," my sister said, with a dreamy, faraway look.

It was a day after the holiday ended, and my sister and I were at our kitchen table. I was preparing to go back to Montreal, back to my routine of morning-to-night Talmud study, back to my friends and to the yeshiva dormitory in which we slept six to a room, with an angry and severe rabbi as dormitory monitor. Danny was still very much on my mind, and I told my sister she'd missed out by not watching *The Chosen* with me.

Robby Benson is soooo good-looking.

"Who?" I asked.

"Robby Benson. He plays Danny."

He plays Danny. Robby Benson. Plays. Danny. Robby. Benson. The words spun in my head, as only the startling truth can.

"He's not Jewish," she said. "He's from Texas."

Robby Benson. Not a Hasid. Not the son of Reb Saunders, who lived in a brownstone in Williamsburg. Not a Hasidic boy with a beaver hat and side curls, with the fringes of his *gartel* flapping by his sides. Not the boy who secretly went to the library to read books about Adler and Jung and Freud.

There was no Danny; it was just a character, and the person behind it had a name, an identity; a goy in Texas—were there even Jews in Texas?—an actor who ate *trayf* and didn't keep Shabbos. And yet, he told Danny's story, which was really the story of every Hasidic boy in Brooklyn who both loved his world and wanted more.

I didn't know how my sister knew this, but she spoke about Robby Benson with puzzling familiarity. I didn't understand my sister's world, didn't know where she got her information from, but in our strictly sex-segregated world, boys and girls lived so completely apart that it felt pointless to inquire. Only later would I learn that my sister and her friends, who weren't obligated with dawn-to-dusk Torah study, occupied themselves with learning about the world. They went shopping, read books, watched movies, and knew the names of the people many Americans talked about. And so she knew about Robby Benson.

Now I wondered: Was it Danny Saunders I wanted to be, or Robby Benson? Did I want my story told, or did I want to act out other people's stories? Or did I want both at once? What was the desire I was afraid to tell even myself?

As I rode the bus back to yeshiva in Montreal, I wondered: Could a Hasid be an actor? I knew of no rule against it, but if we weren't allowed to *watch* movies, would we be allowed to be *in* them?

Probably not.

In the end, I got to be both: Robby Benson and Danny Saunders. Not on a screen or a television set, but in a nightly performance from my top bunk in room number three of our third-floor dormitory. My audience: Moishy Rubin, Sender Gluck, Avrum Yida Schwartz, Chaim Berkowitz, and Mechy Farkash. My five dorm roommates; like me, Hasidic boys from Brooklyn, except they did not have worldly sisters and dead fathers and mothers too filled with grief to care, and they had never watched movies, not a single one.

At night, when Reb Zundel the night monitor left, and the dormitory fell quiet, we would wait, until we heard the large steel door close gently, the dead bolt clack into position. We'd hold our breaths. Faintly, we could hear the sound of Reb Zundel's footfalls going down the stairs, then the outside door creak as it opened, then shut behind him.

"He's gone." It was Moishy who always said it first.

"Wait another minute," Sender would whisper. And we'd wait a few seconds, until Moishy would say, "*Nu,* he's gone," and he'd look up to me from across the room. "Let's hear further."

Sender and Moishy would sit up on their beds, and Avrum Yida would come out from the bunk beneath mine to sit on a chair near the door, wrapping himself in a blanket like a cape. I, from my top bunk, would sit up straight and continue from where I'd left off the night before. I was the narrator of the story and also the actor of every part—Reb Saunders, and Mr. Malter, and Reuven, but most of all, I acted Danny. Confined to my top bunk, all I could do were voices and gesticulations and dramatic head movements. But that was all I needed.

The images of Danny and his world swirled in my head as they came alive in my telling of it all: Danny studying over his Talmud; Danny at bat in the schoolyard, his gleaming blue eyes staring icily at his opponent; Danny at his father's *tisch,* the communal meal with Hasidim all around, singing the famous Satmar "Hakafah Niggun." Danny at the library, Danny at school, Danny in the streets as celebrants cheered the end of the long war and he was suddenly kissed on the mouth by a strange woman. Every scene had been etched in my mind, every word of dialogue fresh, as if I'd heard it only moments earlier.

Deep inside us, there's something called the unconscious!

I would mimic Danny's excited expressions.

It's filled with things that we're afraid to tell even to ourselves!

My audience would be silent, unblinking, barely breathing, it seemed, but every now and then Avrum Yida, on the chair, with his knees up against his chest beneath his blanket, wouldn't be able to contain himself.

"Was it the *real* Satmar 'Hakafah Niggun'?"

"How do they know all these things about us?"

"What does 'the unconscious' mean?"

I fumbled for responses, because I didn't know much more than he did. I, too, had never heard of the unconscious. "It's a psychology thing," I could say only, and Avrum Yida nodded faintly.

I would mimic Danny's father, the rebbe, grilling Reuven on his studies. A Hasid like so many we knew—both severe and good-natured; one moment cruelly mocking his son's friend for misremembering a passage of Talmud, the next moment smiling so warmly at a correct response.

"*Er macht es git, er,*" Moishy Rubin would say with a grin, approving my performance. "He's *good.*"

The others would nod and smile in agreement, and I would

bask in the glow of the small night lamp in the outlet near Sender's bed, in the glow of my friends' approval, in my performance of a boy who was just like me, just like us, who wished for things we, too, might have wished for, if only we knew about them, if they weren't *so deep inside of us* that we were *afraid to tell them even to ourselves*. I imagined what it would be like to be Robby Benson, and we all imagined what it would be like to be Danny, for our dreams to come true, for our stories to be told, until Moishy Rubin's head would fall to his shoulder and his snores would ring through the room, and we knew it was time to save the rest for another night.

JAMIE BRISICK

My Preteen Speed Addiction

He wore white pants, a blue shirt, a red scarf, and a white helmet with a red M on the front. His face was round, boyish. He seemed tangible to my kindergarten mind, a fellow thumb sucker and T-ball whacker, but in fact he was eighteen, a driver on the international racing circuit. His car was white, weapon-looking, with a three-pronged front end. Its name: the Mach 5.

My first celebrity crush was maybe the perfect kind of celebrity crush. He was beyond flesh and blood—he was a cartoon character. I found him every Saturday morning on channel 13. The opening theme song made me salivate with joy.

Here he comes, here comes Speed Racer, he's a demon on wheels . . .

Speed Racer presented a world far more interesting than the one I inhabited. There were high-speed battles against Mammoth Cars and X3s. There was Speed's hot girlfriend, Trixie, and his cool little brother, Spritle, and their pet monkey, Chim Chim, who brought new life to the stuffed monkey I slept with at night. There was Mom and Pops, who showered Speed in love, provided a cozy respite from the dangers that lurked outside. There was that incredible way in which Speed got in and out of his car, a kind of dance/leap/swagger.

Speed bridged me from the Hot Wheels I played with in the living room to the Big Wheel I *vroom-vroom*ed around the neighborhood. My two brothers and I took turns reenacting scenes from the show. We fought over who got to play Speed—pinching, biting, hair-pulling, the occasional mag wheel run over an unsuspecting foot. We negotiated deals. If there was only enough Cap'n Crunch for two bowls, for instance, then whoever got to play Speed had to make do with Dad's Cheerios. Halloween presented a fairly colossal problem that was settled through rock-paper-scissors.

Looking back, it was less about Speed than the forging of a certain kind of relationship. Speed was a hero, a role model, a spur. He taught me how to mimic, how to sublimate. My Big Wheel was not the rain-and-sun-faded hand-me-down from Kevin and Steven; it was the powerful Mach 5. The sidewalk was not a mere strip of pavement at the top of Escalon Drive; it was a racetrack. I was too young to know melancholy and existential dread, but Speed was stirring in me the tools I would later use to combat these things.

And he prepared me for Evel Knievel.

I was six. The training wheels had recently come off my red Huffy bicycle. On *Wide World of Sports* we watched Evel jump nineteen cars. That night, in our bunk beds, my brothers and I replayed every last detail: his star-spangled leathers, his Harley-Davidson XR-750, the blue cape that he discarded before doing the big jump, the way he got us biting our nails and clenching our fists with heebie-jeebies. "How did he get the name Evel?" we debated at length. I figured it was the name his parents gave him. Steven thought it was a nickname. Kevin came up with something vaguely Faustian: "He's broken every bone in his body and he still jumps his motorcycle over nineteen cars? That's beyond human!"

On the following Saturday morning I did not watch *Speed Racer* on channel 13. Instead, I went out to the garage, grabbed a couple scraps of plywood, a few bricks, and every Tonka truck in the bucket. On the sidewalk in front of our house I set up a kind of Evel Knievel miniature: launch and landing ramps with five trucks in between. I remembered that Evel wore protective headgear and ran back into the house to get Dad's aviator sunglasses and Kevin's Notre Dame football helmet.

"C'mon," I called to my brothers, who were playing soccer in the backyard. "You guys gotta see this." They followed me to the front of the house. "That's your seat right there," I told Kevin, pointing to the left side of the Tonka trucks. "And that's yours," I told Steven, pointing to the right.

They sat. I rode a ways up the sidewalk, turned around, and gunned it. But as I got close I hit my brakes, stopping with my front wheel on the ramp. Evel had done this in his nineteen-car jump—a fake-out.

I scratched my crotch, adjusted my glasses, and brought my index finger to my tongue and pointed skyward (I wasn't sure what this last part meant, but I assumed it had something to do with Evel's religious beliefs). I surveyed the three-foot gap and Tonka trucks waiting ominously below. Then I rolled backward, rode two driveways up the block, spun around, and began my approach.

I pedaled hard, my bike rocking back and forth between my legs, my mouth making the *waaaah, waaaah, waaaah* sound of an XR-750. I felt winged. But the instant I hit the ramp it buckled under my weight. Instead of launching skyward like a bird, a plane, a six-year-old Evel Knievel, I crashed head-on into the flotsam of bricks, Tonka trucks, and plywood. My handlebars crossed up and I spilled forward, smacking the pavement with my chin. The sunglasses flew one way, the football helmet—which I'd failed to strap on—the other. Blood splattered my Mickey Mouse T-shirt. I tried my hardest not to cry.

"Where does it hurt?" asked Kevin, borrowing Mom's line.

I pointed to my chin. He escorted me into the house. In the bathroom, Mom smeared away the blood with Betadine. It bubbled and stung.

"Do you think I broke the bone?" I asked hopefully.

"Not quite," she said.

Big Wheels, bicycles, then skateboards. For my eleventh birthday my parents got me a Bahne deck with Chicago trucks and

Cadillac wheels. It had a fabulous glide, but it only really came to life when I discovered *Skateboarder* magazine. The year was 1977. On the west side of Los Angeles a band of teenage skaters known as the Dogtowners tore apart streets, sidewalks, drainage ditches, empty swimming pools, anything smooth and banked. Their pictures in *Skateboarder* captivated me. I wanted to skate like them; I wanted to look like them. Most of the Dogtowners were poor kids from broken homes. They dressed like Jeff Spicoli.

Vans deck shoes—navy blue
Tube socks all frayed and stretched out
OP corduroy shorts with boxers hanging out the bottoms
Levi's corduroy pants, two sizes too big
Surf T-shirts (Blue Cheer, Natural Progression, Zephyr,
        Mr. Zog's Sex Wax)

This was what my back-to-school clothes list looked like. What my loving mother did not know was that I took my spankin'-new gear out to the street and scraped it on the pavement to get it looking more "Dogtownerish." Tony Alva wore a pimpin' porkpie hat, Shogo Kubo wore a rising-sun headband. I wore both.

Watching the Dogtowners in the surf movie *Go for It* was a real treat, but skating with them at Kenter Elementary School in Brentwood truly lit up my world. They possessed an insouciance, a flow, an inner music. I studied every last detail: the way they hopped the fence like panthers, held their boards as if they were rifles, pushed three times, then charged down the blacktop bank in a low tuck, knock-kneed, hands like Merlin the spellcaster. They carved up and down, up and down, drawing graceful, poetic lines, crossing-stepping to the nose here, ducking into an imaginary tube there. It was exactly the kind of projecting I was familiar with. They were riding the concrete bank as if it were a wave. In their heads they were surfing.

Skateboarding led me to surfing, surfing led me to three West Coast titles and a sponsorship from Quiksilver. I turned pro in 1986, did five years on the world tour. Pictures of me were in the surf mags. I signed autographs on the beaches of Rio, Biarritz, Bondi, Cape Town. And even when I was at the top of my game I was still a mimicker and a hero worshipper. Before paddling out against the very pros I was trying to beat—and sometimes did—I studied their acts the way I studied Speed Racer on television at age five (Gary Elkerton scraped his toes on the sand like a bull about to be let loose in a ring; Tom Curren shuffled hips, cracked knuckles).

And don't let's get started on this writing business. I'm a forty-eight-year-old man-child bouncing to the characters in fiction, emulating the writers and comedians I admire, still mimicking consciously and unconsciously. Not that I haven't tapped my own inner voice, but more like that voice enjoys dancing around in other people's shoes. I find that the monotony of yet another sunny day in Los Angeles can take on a happier hue if I imagine myself as The Dude from *The Big Lebowski*. Stuff that torments me, scares me, ties my stomach in knots—I think what Louis CK would do with it and it somehow lightens.

Not long ago I was giving a reading at a literary festival in Cornwall, England. It was a difficult passage about a close friend of mine who drowned while surfing in giant waves. I started improvising, telling the story as I remembered it, when suddenly I was seized by a combination of raw emotion and stage fright. I completely lost my train of thought. A hot flash washed over my face, my palms got sweaty; I froze up. And then George Carlin stepped in. In "Fart Jokes" he doesn't so much crescendo as he simply runs out of material. "I have no ending for this," he says/I said, "so I take a small bow."

This lineage of inspirational figures, these lives that have given spirit and sparkle to my own, all trace back to Speed.

PART 5

Finally, We Meet

When you're younger, your fantasies and those first crazy pangs of longing and unarticulated lust seem so real, but they are light-years away from reality. Often, your feelings about your object of affection simply play out in your head like a Technicolor movie. But sometimes you go *really* far to meet an actual crush. Sometimes you happen upon your crush in the unlikeliest of settings. Either way, what happens when perception and reality come crashing together and you come face-to-face with your first celebrity crush later in life?

Newman's Own

I know the moment I see him rising like Poseidon out of the inky sea that he's the One. He looks like a god—bronzed, lean, muscular, with eyes so blue you can't believe they're real. Everyone on shore defers to him, and it's no wonder: here is a man you can rely on, a man who will never let you down, a man with the power to save you from anything, including yourself.

It doesn't matter that he's a character in an epic film played by a famous movie star. Or that I'm a gawky thirteen-year-old with giant buckteeth and wads of scratchy toilet paper stuffed in my training bra. I believe that when we meet our connection will be cosmic, a Big Bang of love so shattering, so filled with rapture, that my tiny breasts and big choppers will be of little consequence. I also believe that the actor, Paul Newman, and the character, Ari Ben Canaan in *Exodus,* are exactly the same person.

My soul mate.

I'm ready to turn my life over to him, quit junior high school, say good riddance to my childhood, including my clueless parents and my brother—the traitor, who has gone off to college and deserted me—and all the other people who think they know me but don't. I am ready to be *seen*. And set ablaze by love.

Which is why I find myself twisted like a frozen pretzel on the steps of St. Ignatius Loyola church on a biting-cold Saturday in February. Paul lives directly across the street. He doesn't know

I'm here, waiting for him—or even that I exist. But he will—if not today, then soon.

In January, after the movie was released, I read in one of my mother's fashion magazines that Paul has an apartment on Park Avenue. A few days later I took the train in from Westchester and launched my mission to find his building by asking every single doorman starting at Fifty-Ninth Street if he lived there. Most of them shook their heads and looked at me like I was some kind of crazy bananas kid. But two weeks into my search, the miracle happened. The stout uniformed sentry at 1000 Park winked at me and whispered in my ear, "Promise you won't tell nobody."

I promised.

Before I saw *Exodus*—the 1960 blockbuster based on the runaway bestseller by Leon Uris—I was a lonely but spunky girl with vague dreams of a becoming an actress on Broadway. Still, my main role model up to that point had been Anne Frank, so I was unsure of my future. Should I carry the torch she lit and become a writer instead? Then I saw the movie. In *Exodus* there are teenagers who escaped the death camps who look so robust, so joyful and spirited, that it's obvious I belong among them—a kibbutznik, singing and dancing, working in the fields, living communally, no parents in sight. The older ones fall madly, hungrily, in love. It's also obvious that I would be a much better match for Paul than that wan, Waspy, milquetoasty Eva Marie Saint.

I am in love with this sweeping alternative to my dreary, middle-class, suburban life. In my new life my mother won't be around to pester me daily, "Honey, are you *sure* you don't want to get a nose job?" No one gets nose jobs where I'm going. Where I'm going big noses are a symbol of pride, not shame.

Shivering on the steps of St. Ignatius Loyola, I imagine the moment when Paul and I will first meet. He's walking briskly up Park, his cheeks flushed pink from the wind. I'm standing on the third step up from the street so he doesn't notice how short I am.

"Hello," I say—or possibly, "Shalom." Just a simple one-word greeting. Even though I read that he hates to be recognized and goes out of his way to dodge his fans, some mysterious force makes him stop and turn in my direction. "Hello" (or "Shalom"), he replies in his achingly familiar, sweetly gravelly voice. At first he's puzzled, disoriented, surprising himself that he's stopped to talk to me. I don't say anything else. Words would be too gross, too inadequate to capture the momentousness of the moment. I just stand there, smiling. Then he takes a step closer and bores right through me with those world-famous cobalt eyes. That's when he realizes I'm the One. Even though he's completely devoted to Joanne and until this second took it on faith that she was the One. Even though in all their years of marriage he has never strayed once. Even though I'm just this goofy girl who appears out of nowhere.

This is the scene I replay in my mind to keep me going until it's time to hop on the Lexington Avenue bus down to Grand Central to catch the train back to Westchester before it gets dark. Still, I'm determined. I take up my post the following Saturday and two or three Saturdays after that. But each week I leave disappointed and nearly frostbitten. I get a terrible cold. Even though I still love him, still believe that if only we could meet we'd have something really special, I grow disheartened and frustrated and decide to take a break from my weekly stakeouts.

I don't know it then, but it will take twenty-eight more years before Paul and I are in the same place at the same time.

By the time I outgrow my training bra and its toilet-tissue stuffing, I realize that my imagined romance with Paul was a childish fantasy. On the other hand, my imagined romance with his clone—a fearless hunk who looks and behaves like Ari Ben Canaan in the movie but is an actual person—is very much alive. So is my dream of living on a kibbutz, and all the free love, folk dancing, and socialist solidarity that go with it. Still, I have to wait until I'm eighteen, the summer after my freshman year at NYU, before I'm old enough to sign up for an eight-week program called Summer in Kibbutz.

When I say good-bye to my parents at JFK before boarding the El Al plane to Tel Aviv, I don't mention that I won't be returning at the end of the summer. I don't mention that I plan to find my soul mate on the kibbutz and live out my dream.

Founded by British Zionists in 1948, the year after Israel was granted statehood by the United Nations, Kibbutz Kfar-Hanassi is in the northern Galilee overlooking the Jordan River, within an easy grenade toss of the Golan Heights. I learn how vulnerable we are my first full day on the kibbutz when I oversleep and miss the four thirty A.M. truck that takes volunteers to the *matah*—the orchard—where I'm supposed to be picking apples. I have to walk there instead, only I get lost and find myself on a cliff looking across the Jordan at a couple of Syrian soldiers with machine guns pointed right at me.

Terrified, I run as fast as I can back in the direction I came from and eventually stumble upon the orchard. I feel like a fuckup, and the morning's upsetting wrong turn foreshadows the rest of the trip.

Here's what happens. An endless stream of Israeli men are more than happy to sleep with me. Most of them are dark and swarthy, but there's one very handsome, flaxen-haired, blue-eyed Sabra (native-born Israeli) that I have my eye on. At first he doesn't notice me, but then—O, be still my beating heart!—he does. We spend quite a few steamy sleepless nights together, even though by the end of each day I'm so exhausted from the heat and the manual labor, I can barely stay awake. Still, I force myself to rally and put out because I'm sure that Dov, my Sabra, is the Paul doppelgänger I've been grooming myself for ever since I saw *Exodus*. I'm ready to pledge myself to him and I'm pretty sure he feels the same way— until the night he dumps me for another summer girl, a blonde who is taller and bustier than I am.

Things continue to slide downhill. My roommate Karen and I score some hashish from an Israeli hippie in Tiberias, a pretty town by the Sea of Galilee. We have fun sneaking out and getting stoned behind the pool at night, certain that no one is onto us. Then one day when we return from lunch we find two policemen waiting for us in our concrete hut, one of them fingering our stash. Clearly, some upstanding kibbutznik has sniffed and squealed. In the car on the way to the police station, Karen and I manage to concoct a story. We tell the cops we think the brown sticky stuff is incense, which we unwittingly accepted from some Arab guy in Acre. This results in a field trip to Acre with the cops. We spend an entire day under a blazing sun scouring the town in search of a man who doesn't exist. We look at lineups and mug shots. We comb the narrow streets and teeming souk. The cops pressure us to identify someone—anyone—but we're not completely lacking in integrity or principles, so we resist. On the bus ride back to the kibbutz, the cops try to feel us up, then beg us to spend the night with them in the police station. We refuse.

In Israel in 1966, pretty much everyone is having sex with everyone else. Still, there's no Paul, no Ari, no worthy runner-up contenders, no more fever dream of my romantic Zionist life.

Twenty-eight years after my unsuccessful stakeouts on Park Avenue, I'm riding down in an elevator in Madison Square Garden after a horse show. This elevator is so enormous it could accommodate teams of horses, but tonight it is stuffed with people, mostly middle-aged women who love horses. I'm with my husband—well, okay, my third husband, but the good one, the keeper—and he is smooshed up against the double doors, facing into the elevator. When it slows to a stop one floor down, discontent ripples through the packed car. As it is, we're already a little too intimate for comfort; there isn't room for one more passenger. Then the doors open and we gasp a collective gasp. It's *him*. Paul. Of course: his daughter was riding in the show. Everyone backs up and presses flesh against flesh even tighter to try to make room—that is, everyone except the one passenger who is not looking in Paul's direction, the passenger who is body-blocking his entrance. My husband—the oblivious recipient of a sea of murderous looks as the double doors close.

Someone has the presence of mind to press the button for the next floor down and when the elevator stops, a stampede of women, including me, rushes headlong out of the car and up the stairs one level so we can wait for the next elevator and ride down with him. But by the time we get there, like a phantom, he's vanished.

If I didn't love him so much, I, too, might have been tempted to murder my husband for botching the moment I've been waiting for most of my life. But, later, after I calm down, it occurs to me that maybe it's better this way. Maybe it's better if my path and Paul's never cross, better if our eyes never meet. Because if they did, I realize with the perspective of someone who is forty, not thirteen or eighteen, someone who no longer yearns desperately to be saved, it's unlikely we would share that cosmic Big Bang of rapture I'd been banking on as a kid.

And so with my girlish dreams safely intact, in some alternate universe Paul Newman will always be mine.

SAM WEISMAN

The Captain

Kareem Abdul-Jabbar, formerly Lew Alcindor. We've always been linked cosmically, ever since that week in April 1947 when we were both born in New York State, two hundred miles apart, him in New York City and me in the quiet little upstate city of Binghamton. His parents were tall and African American, mine were short and Jewish, but we were both raised in loving middle-class households. We were both taught the importance of hard work, education, and morality, and we both grew up around music. Most important, the two of us were influenced by fathers who told us tales of wars and hard times. We were truly baby boomers and had a lot in common.

At some point, during elementary school, Lew and I, in our own separate worlds, started to bounce a basketball, shoot hoops anywhere we could, and fantasize about making the winning shot. That's when our cosmic paths diverged. He went on to be a graceful seven-foot giant, revolutionizing the game of basketball and making countless winning shots, while I went on to continue being short and Jewish, like my parents. I don't recall ever making a winning shot.

I first became aware of him in 1963. The basketball phenomenon Lew Alcindor was dominating New York City high school basketball, starring at Power Memorial Academy, a private Catholic school that won three straight city championships while he played there. I read about Alcindor in the pages of basketball journals like

Street & Smith magazine and the *Sporting News,* even occasionally in the *New York Times.* I steadfastly followed his incredible exploits as he scored 2,067 points during his high school career, leading Power to a 79-2 record and a national championship.

At that time, I was a distinctly less famous baller, playing an unnoticed and earthbound game as a junior varsity shooting guard at Deerfield Academy, a boarding school in western Massachusetts. Our varsity was really good, and I consoled myself for not making the team with the knowledge that a couple of our players were featured in the same basketball magazines as Lew Alcindor. Nevertheless, I hung around the gym, trying to get better and longing to be part of the basketball community. I wanted to be like the varsity guys. I wanted to be like Lew.

Being a scholarship student, taking a weekend away from Deerfield was a big event. In my junior year, I was lucky enough to go to New York City with a couple of classmates who were from there. At some point during the visit, I was meant to meet up with a friend at a landmark made famous by J. D. Salinger, one of our heroes of the time. My schoolmate, who had grown up in the city, and who was way more sophisticated than me, instructed me to rendezvous with him "under the clock at the Biltmore."

The Biltmore Hotel was classic old New York. I entered nervously, dressed in my best prep school outfit—blue blazer, gray slacks, button-down shirt, striped tie, and penny loafers. A significant part of my life as a poor kid in an elite private school was about trying to fit in. Looking around the imposing lobby that day, as I waited for my buddy, I studied all the "important" people, rushing to connect with other "important" people. Where was I headed in my life? Would I ever be "important"? Did it even matter?

My Holden Caulfield–like reverie was broken. I saw someone, impossibly tall, incredibly smooth, strolling through the Biltmore lobby, heading toward the clock. It was Alcindor. He was dressed similarly to me, but the midsixties style looked sharper on him, more at home on his lanky frame. He paced around for a bit, looking at his watch. Clearly he was there to meet someone *hugely* important—perhaps a journalist who would write a major article about the young star. Would I see the piece when it came out? Before the Internet, it took so much more dedication to be a fan. Alcindor seemed like me in some ways—smart and sensitive. He was just taller, and famous. Could we be friends? Pen pals? I wanted to go up to him and engage in conversation, but as I tried to summon up the courage, he abruptly left the lobby, and my chance was gone.

They still had newsreels in movie theaters back then, and usually sports highlights were included. I recall seeing the young Alcindor dominate the tough New York City prep basketball world with his incredible big-man skills, ruling the court with strength, speed, and remarkable grace, playing the "city game" above the rim. In brief black-and-white interview clips, the teenage Alcindor appeared thoughtful, poised, and focused in a fashion way beyond his years. He seemed so cool, wearing his Power Memorial sweats, standing next to his "old-school" coach, Jack Donohue.

The incredible freedom and creativity of the clips showing Alcindor on the court were a strange juxtaposition with the shots of him and his coach. The middle-aged Irish white guy smiled, arm around the waist of the African American giant responsible for bringing unprecedented attention to his high school basketball team, and he reveled in the moment. In retrospect, there was something in this image that was prescient. An older white man standing next to a powerful young black man, in a slightly awkward pose—in a certain way, that was indicative of the calm before the storm that was about to take place in the 1960s.

With way less fanfare than would take place today, Lew Alcindor made the decision in 1965 to attend UCLA and play for the great coach John Wooden. The highlights of his UCLA career are the stuff of legends: three NCAA championships, the famous forty-seven-game unbeaten streak, three-time All-American, and the first-ever Naismith Player of the Year win. But there were negatives as well. The NCAA couldn't seem to embrace the quiet force Alcindor displayed on the court. In an effort to temper his dominance, after his initial varsity season (freshmen were not allowed on the varsity back then), the college rules were altered to outlaw the dunk. The powers that be wanted to level the playing field.

It was how Lew responded to this obstacle that distinguished him and made me admire him even more. He developed the distinctive "sky hook," the shot that remained his signature for his entire playing career. This balletic, impossible-to-block shot was a perfect statement for the man and for the time—an out-of-the-box gesture that couldn't be forgotten. One could imagine a highlight reel of the collegiate Alcindor scored to a montage of sixties music—Hendrix, Joplin, the Who, and Buffalo Springfield. Lew was saying: "This is me! I'm here to stay. The world is changing; try to stop us." He grew an Afro, protested politically, smoked pot, and met with Muslim leaders, showing that he openly was going to stand up to "the man." There was no concern about what others thought of him. Lew Alcindor was the greatest college basketball player of his time, and at the same moment he was fully engaged with many of his peers in one of the greatest cultural revolutions the country had ever experienced.

It was still the dark ages media-wise, and the opportunities to watch UCLA basketball on the East Coast, where I was in college, were limited. But when I did get to see Lew's games on television, or when I read about him in newspapers and magazines, I recall images of him engaged in seemingly intense conversations with Coach Wooden. The unlikely pairing of this young giant from the big city and the middle-aged, straitlaced Hoosier became destined to make sports history.

Wooden knew how to manage the Alcindor phenomenon, and Lewis (as Wooden always called him) gave himself over to his coach and UCLA's quest for greatness. In turn, the coach struggled with the rapidly changing manners of the sixties. Alcindor and many of his teammates sported long hair and experimented with illegal substances. Wooden knew that the changes in the world around him made up a powerful force. That force could not be tempered, so it had to be embraced. He trusted Lewis to do the right thing when it mattered most, and he was not disappointed. They represented the essence of the father-son relationship, a relationship I felt strongly playing sports as a young man.

Many years later, in a 1992 *Los Angeles Times* article on Alcindor's UCLA scoring record being eclipsed, Wooden was quoted: "I talked to him once and said, 'I'm sure that we could devise an offense to make you the all-time leading scorer in college history, but if we do that, we're not going to win national championships.' . . . I'll never forget it—he said, 'Coach, you know I wouldn't want that.'"

This was the ultimate team player.

Alcindor's quest for his path in life had led him to convert to the Muslim faith while in college, and he now decided to change his name to Kareem Abdul-Jabbar. The meaning of his new name was "Noble Servant of the Mighty One." It felt like being a transformative professional basketball player wasn't enough for him. He needed to continue a process that was searching for a higher meaning, and in that search he always seemed to be making a bridge from the past to the present. His game was modern, and so was his life.

I made my own leap in my life, but it took me more than a decade of struggle. During those years, I lost touch with my Lewis/Kareem fandom and threw off the traditional expectations of what my life should be. After being educated in boarding school and at Yale, I dedicated myself to a career in the arts, becoming an actor. Really, I was more of a waiter/bartender while I studied and waited for my "big break."

During those years, my basketball jones was rekindled in countless pickup games. I began to mature physically and emotionally, and that development nudged me forward. My basketball game developed as well. I somehow saw the court better and actually understood the creativity of the sport, sensing a link between athletic performance and the work of the actor. Work started to come, and I found myself in Hollywood, making a living as an actor and once again becoming obsessed with basketball.

By this time, Kareem was ensconced in Los Angeles as well, having been traded to the Lakers, and becoming a show business figure in his own right following a legendary cameo as Roger Murdock in the film classic *Airplane!* It so impressed me that this guy could squeeze himself into that movie role, get laughs, and still retain his Zen-like dignity. Kareem, in my view, both on the court and off, defined the correct balance of ego and esteem: he saw himself in the same way that others saw him. That was my struggle as a young actor, and I admired Kareem for his ability to be so centered.

Now married, I dragged my wife, Constance, to see the Lakers play, wanting her to understand all the nuances of the game. We became season-ticket holders and went to a majority of the games at the old Fabulous Forum. The franchise was a bit at sea, having never recovered from the glory days of the West/Baylor/Wilt/Goodrich years. Kareem had been expected to deliver more championships, but he was never surrounded with the right supporting cast. The media habitually criticized him for his inability to galvanize the team, as well as for his increasingly quiet demeanor. To me it appeared he might be losing interest in the game. I felt for him, because I viewed him as a fellow artist. He was a team guy first, despite all the MVP awards and the amazing individual stats. If he couldn't pursue his art in the right way, was it even worth pursuing?

Then, in 1979, with the first pick in the NBA draft, the Lakers drafted Earvin "Magic" Johnson, and the doldrums in L.A. abruptly ended. For the next ten years, my life revolved around watching a rejuvenated Kareem join with Magic and a rotating "Showtime" cast of stars and role players to rock the Fabulous Forum with winning seasons. The fans were insane, by laid-back Southern California standards. We sang along to Randy Newman's "I Love L.A.," adored

Chick Hearn's play-by-play on radio and television, and made fun of all the celebrities jumping on colorful owner Jerry Buss's bandwagon. Laker basketball was "the scene," the Forum Club was the place to be, and my man Kareem, the cerebral, cool, and sensitive veteran, continued his amazing ride at the center of it all, even high-fiving super fan Jack Nicholson courtside.

Magic called Kareem "the Captain," respecting his stature on the team and in the league, while he orchestrated some of the most exciting basketball the world had ever seen. I loved the fact that Kareem always referred to Magic as "Earvin" when he spoke about him, not using his nickname and displaying a distinctive fatherly tone. Once again, Kareem was acting as a bridge from one era to the next, while he solidified his place as one of the greatest players to ever play the game.

I attended Kareem's last game, on April 23, 1989, a few days after he had celebrated his forty-second birthday. My seven-year-old son, Dan, was with me, as was my two-year-old daughter, Meg. The retirement ceremony brought tears to my eyes. I stood, holding my kids, applauding the Captain, as the fans bade farewell to the leading scorer in the history of the NBA. He settled into the Kareem-sized rocking chair the team gave him as a gift, and everyone present knew that there would never be another like him.

Lewis was the essential athlete of my generation, and for over twenty-five years I had admired him. The Depression and World War II had defined our parents and shaped how they raised us. We grew up looking for our own benchmarks as our heroes were assassinated, our stature in the world was threatened, and we became immersed in the digital revolution. During all that time, Kareem represented those values and continued to play the game of basketball the right way—with class and grace.

I transitioned from acting to directing in the eighties and I was given the chance to direct my first feature film with Disney's *D2: The Mighty Ducks*. Though it was a film about hockey, I somehow justified working a scene into the film for my favorite basketball player. Kareem was approached about appearing as himself, and he accepted. I was going to spend the day with my crush!

The location was an incredible beach house in Malibu, and in addition to Kareem, we cast three NHL stars of the time—Cam Neely, Luc Robitaille, and Chris Chelios—as well as Olympians Kristi Yamaguchi and Greg Louganis. We were shooting a party sequence, and the athletes played themselves in short scenes with the film's star, Emilio Estevez, and our screenwriter Steve Brill, playing a slick sports agent.

Thrilled to be in the presence of so many sports greats, I ran around like more of a host than a director, until later in the day, when I noticed Kareem sitting quietly off to the side, reading, while we were in the midst of a lighting setup. This was my moment. I sat down next to him, and we began talking. It had been thirty years since that afternoon under the clock at the Biltmore. But the truly great thing was that we had a lot more to talk about at forty-six than we would have at sixteen.

I was nervous and wanted to maintain a director-like demeanor, but I don't think I did. This was the great Lew Alcindor. I had followed him for three decades, growing up with him from afar, and I told him how thrilled I was to finally meet him. He smiled and said, "Thanks, I appreciate it." He then grew quiet. We were sitting in the bright sunlight of a glorious Malibu day, and he was wearing shades, so it was hard to sense his mood.

After a second, he continued: "Being a director is kind of like being a coach, isn't it?" I agreed completely. Kareem went on: "I like the way you work with all the actors and the crew. It feels like a good team." He paused and thought for a second, then said, "That's nice." We continued talking, about movies, basketball, people we knew, and life. It was nice.

KIMBERLY DAWN NEUMANN

Dance with Me?

He had me jumping, spinning, kicking, twirling, and sweating. Everything about this man was perfection in my baby ballerina eyes.

I don't remember when Mikhail Baryshnikov first found his way onto my radar, though I was probably about ten years old. I might have first seen a photo or read about him in *Dance Magazine* . . . or maybe I'd seen him dance on a PBS special? Regardless of where I caught my first glimpse, I can't remember a time when I didn't worship this demigod of dance. When it came to a man who could do multiple pirouettes while effortlessly winning female hearts with his piercing blue eyes, he was in a class all his own.

It wasn't his obvious sex appeal that first grabbed my attention. I was too young to comprehend that. But what I did understand and always have was the concept of extreme physicality. I was training hours per day by the time I was a teen, and of one thing I was sure . . . this man could move, and it moved me.

With a spectacular gravity-defying leap or gentle extension of his arm, he could take my breath away. Through his body he was able to capture everything I imagined that a person might feel in love . . . because to me, love and dance were intertwined. Dancers get this and sacrifice their bodies for it. In my world, Baryshnikov was passion personified.

My mother, Donna, says I came out of the womb dancing. It wasn't a choice. It's who I am. Dance has always been an intrinsic part of my life and how I define myself. When people ask me what I do, my response has always been "I am a dancer" first and foremost. Not "I dance." It's deeper than that. It's my soul.

Gregory Hines—with whom Baryshnikov would later collaborate—got it right when he said, "I don't remember not dancing. When I realized I was alive and these were my parents, and I could walk and talk, I could dance."

With all this in mind, it would make perfect sense that the only real celebrity crush I can recall growing up was of that same breed (yes, dancers are a breed). I ate, slept, dreamed, and bled for dance. It's an obsession for those who must do it. The countless hours of training that go into perfecting the craft, the determination, the sacrifice . . . they all happen because of love. So when someone is really, really good at that . . . they become an object of adulation.

Most young dancers will tell you that there isn't a lot of time for other things once you head down that path toward professional. There is a discipline involved with dance that means your life becomes very regimented. My daily schedule started with my getting up before six A.M. of my own volition to practice at the barre my dad had installed downstairs in our home. I wanted to be good so badly I would even attach ankle weights to my legs while I did grand battements in an attempt to get my legs higher when I kicked, and I would tuck my feet under the couch and point with all my might to make my arches look better.

Then, after a full day of school, my mom would put me in the car and drive me an hour each way from our foothills home in Evergreen, Colorado, to Denver so I could train (bless my parents for affording me the opportunity to chase my dreams and enhance my dancing gifts). Of course, that was until I turned sixteen, and on that day, Mom took me to the Department of Motor Vehicles and said I was staying there until I passed so I could drive myself to all my classes. Fortunately I did it on the first try (typical of a type A dancer).

At around that age, other interests began to develop for me

as well. I was exceptionally naïve—probably because of my intense focus on ballet more than boys—but the awareness was there, and not long after, I experienced my first kiss in the parking lot of the local library . . . coincidentally, right next to the DMV where I had been given vehicular freedom only months earlier. The baby ballerina was growing up.

When I finally saw the movie *The Turning Point*, my crush on Baryshnikov went in a whole new direction. The movie had been out for years by the time I was allowed a viewing; more adult content had meant that it was previously off-limits to a very young dancer, but as a teenager, the reins were loosened. And oh, did my heart swoon at the sight of Baryshnikov as Yuri in that film. I wanted more than anything to be Leslie Browne's character Emilia—not only because of the way it must have felt to dance with a partner like him, but because of the way he seduced her. Dancing à deux can be incredibly intimate and sensual. It's like foreplay all by itself, and watching that was titillating for a "trina." I will never forget the scene where Yuri had just finished rehearsing with Emilia and you saw him kiss her and then close the door. I don't know what I thought happened behind that closed door (again, remember . . . exceptionally naïve at sixteen), but I knew it had to have something to do with, well . . . a different kind of dance.

At that point, all you had to do was say the name Baryshnikov and I melted. I also loved his movie *White Nights*—in which Baryshnikov starred with Gregory Hines—and listened to the original motion picture soundtrack endlessly while most kids my age were listening to Madonna.

Then the unthinkable happened. I found out Baryshnikov was coming to my home state of Colorado with a troupe of dancers to perform. I couldn't even imagine seeing him dance live. He was this huge icon and I knew I lived in a small town far away from the bright lights of the fashionable world in which I imagined he thrived. Though the tickets were expensive, somehow my parents found the funds to get my mom and me into the audience. I didn't even care when someone at the performance spilled his drink on me; I was transfixed. I wanted to dance with this man more than anything in the world. I had no idea how I was supposed to make it happen, but I just knew in my heart that it had to be thrilling.

Fast-forward about five years. I opted not to go into a ballet company out of high school. Instead, I chose to pursue my degree in journalism from the University of Maryland since academia had also been important to me (I graduated valedictorian of my high school class) while dancing professionally as a contract dancer for the Washington National Opera at the Kennedy Center. I knew I was still going to dance for a living, but I shifted my focus from pure ballet to musical theater. Upon graduation, I moved to New York City and started to audition.

It was tough. I struggled to make ends meet, lived in a closet-sized apartment with two roommates, and sometimes wondered how I would survive in the city. But then I would go to dance class and find myself surrounded by some of the most incredible dancers I'd ever seen and I'd be inspired all over again. It was worth it because I couldn't imagine my life playing out any other way.

One day about a year after I'd arrived in Manhattan, I headed to Steps on Seventy-Fourth Street and Broadway—a popular New York City dance studio—to take ballet from a teacher there whose style I favored. I climbed up the grimy back stairwell because the elevator was taking too long that morning, paid my $15 for class, and slipped into my oh-so-familiar shoes. The studio was bright with high ceilings and a lot of light, but musty owing to the dancers whose blood, sweat, and possibly tears had been collected in the hour before I got there. I headed to the barre, knowing my place in that world, and began to stretch. Then my heart stopped.

In walked Baryshnikov. To take class. With me.

I actually felt my legs begin to shake when he smiled directly at me and placed himself at the same barre. This couldn't really be happening, could it? I mean, there he was . . . the man I had dreamed about dancing with forever.

As the pianist began to play the familiar chords of the opening plié music, I tried to get my heart rate under control and to focus.

Calm down.

I remember attempting to pay attention to my own body and to think about the work I was doing. But I couldn't fully concentrate. I was trying not to stare at him going through the same motions as me at the barre, but how could I not watch? His technique was stunning, his body under exquisite control, his blue eyes . . . beautiful. And he was so close I could touch him.

The rest of that class went by in a blur. But I was left with the realization that I had done it. I had danced with Baryshnikov. Maybe not in the way I'd fantasized about, but at that moment all the years of hard work I had put in to get to that advanced level—a level that would allow me to be in a class with arguably one of the most iconic male dancers ever—well, it felt worth it.

I would go on to have a terrific career that allowed me to perform on Broadway in shows like the revival of *A Chorus Line, Annie Get Your Gun,* and *Ragtime;* in TV/film; and on stages all over the country and world.

But I will forever think of that one random day in a light-filled dance studio in NYC as the moment I made it.

Never in a million years did I think I would actually end up dancing with Baryshnikov, and I did. I remember calling my mom in tears as I left the dance studio that day to let her know my dream had come true.

Because on that beautiful spring day in New York City, Baryshnikov had left me jumping, spinning, kicking, twirling, and sweating. For real.

Oh, Mary!

Even as a boy of six, I knew Laura Petrie had more going on than the Mom Thing. The suburban moms on my block did not wear black capris, did not fill out a sweater like that, did not jazz dance. They didn't have that smile. They did not delectably sob to their husbands, "Oh, Dick!" "Oh, Jack!" "Oh, Stan"—their lamentations a kind of seduction.

Laura was the original MILF, which to my latent-stage mind stood for "Mom I'd Like to Hug," and later "Mom I'd Like to Marry," and never anything disgusting, never anything involving the flesh or fluids. Ours was a pure, single-beds kind of love.

I would be a Rob to her Laura, a professional comedy writer with a beautiful, limber wife, one whose wacky shenanigans I would instantly forgive with a rubbery smile and a hug.

A good long hug.

And so I imprinted on Mrs. Petrie, and she became my female template, the model for many real-life loves to come, from my high school crush on a one-year-older woman, forever unrequited, to a college crush requited more than a decade later, and into adulthood. It is not much of a coincidence that my wife and my most serious past girlfriend each used the same photo of Laura Petrie as their avatar on their Facebook page without the other one knowing. I never got either of them to sob properly (sweet, funny, not my fault), and my one attempt at tripping over an ottoman resulted in a back injury that plagues me to this day.

To be clear: my crush was on Laura Petrie and not Mary Tyler

Moore. When the actress reemerged in the seventies as Mary Richards, I wasn't much interested. She was funny and lovable and all that. But she was too skinny for my adolescent tastes—I was into Rhodas—and, it seemed, she was always dating losers named Larry. And then later, in *Ordinary People,* she played a maternal monster who drove her son to attempt suicide. She was brilliant but not what you'd call hot (a MILK, if you will). After watching her destroy poor Timothy Hutton, I transferred my celebrity crush to his savior, the angelic and impossibly pretty Elizabeth McGovern, where it stayed for a number of years. (Also not quite coincidentally, my wife's most serious past boyfriend later dated Elizabeth's sister.)

Yet some part of me always wanted a wife who would accidentally open an inflatable lifeboat in the middle of the living room. And so Laura Petrie burned on in my child heart, eternal as she was in reruns, and I never let go of the conviction that I would one day make her my bride, or mother, either or both.

As luck—no, fate—would have it, in 1992 I found myself in a television greenroom with Mary Tyler Moore. I was thirty-four; she was fifty-six, my age now. She had not yet overdone the surgical maintenance and looked great. Also in the greenroom was Julia Louis-Dreyfus, still *Seinfeld* cute and not yet *Veep* stunning. As a writer on the show they were appearing on, I was essentially invisible, and so they spoke freely.

Julia had recently had a baby. She began talking about the difficulties she was having breast-feeding, which is not the kind of talk a single guy in his thirties typically encounters. The problem, she said, was that her nipples were getting cracked, and they were bleeding.

And then:

"Yeah, cracked nipples; those are the worst," Mary Tyler Moore said.

It became impossible to imagine Laura Petrie and not see her cracked, bleeding nipples as she wailed, "Oh, Rob!"

It was over between us.

DAVE SINGLETON

I Think I Love Him

His hair made me swoon long before I'd heard that expression. I didn't know the word "perfection," either. But when I was nine (to be precise, nine years and eight days), I grasped what it meant.

I had no adequate words then to describe how I felt when I first saw David Cassidy in *The Partridge Family,* which premiered September 25, 1970. I just knew it was the best birthday present I received that year. After a month of alluring television previews, there he was, on-screen, dressed in red velvet pants and vest with white shirt, strumming his guitar and singing onstage.

Teen magazines were quick to zero in on his unfussy yet perfectly symmetrical shag haircut, parted on the side, with beautiful chestnut-brown waves cascading over his forehead like a follicle waterfall and sweeping behind his head like sea grass in the ocean breeze of an eternal summer. His smile was easy yet complicated—I identified with the longing I saw behind it. He wore beatnik-chic bell-bottom jeans that rode low over what seemed like no hips at all. His look fell on the sartorial scale somewhere between Hardy Boys and Woodstock hippie. Often, he wore his shirt open several buttons, exposing a smooth tan chest, sometimes with a puka-shell necklace framing his throat. And his voice—so smooth and pleading, wanting to connect, openhearted but not too flashy.

I see now how this romantic ideal imprinted on my soul like the first chords of an unforgettable song rooting you to a newly discovered desire within yourself. What I didn't know at nine was that I'd made an unassailable commitment to its enduring power, and that I would have an inchoate longing to reconnect to it, always. But I'm getting ahead of myself.

My family had recently moved back from Pittsburgh, Pennsylvania, to Alexandria, Virginia, and I was having a hard time adjusting to my new school, an uptight and conservative Episcopalian haven for boys, many of whose parents were showy and well-to-do, which mine decidedly were not. It was the kind of place that fought with all the cavalry they could muster the onslaught of liberalism in the form of a half-credit art course. With uniforms, strict policies, tough male teacher-coaches, and a smattering of bitter old nun wannabes who ruled, literally, with thick wooden yardsticks they weren't afraid to smack an errant note-passing boy's hand with, it might as well have been Catholic school. The focus was on football, math, science, and God—in that order.

I had no voice in that classroom and felt like a prisoner at home. I was the youngest of four children, the other three of whom were nearly a decade older, the three of them being whatever you'd call the WASP equivalent of Irish triplets—perhaps just ambitious. The triumvirate was born to middle-class, aspiring parents who embodied post–World War II dreams and expectations of perfection. Later, they spoke of how our father, wearing a chef's hat, manning the grill with martini in hand, would proudly exclaim, "Don't we have the life?" during weekend barbecues. It was a time when children were seen and not heard. A family's dirty laundry was safely tucked away, at least until the mid-1960s, when the 1950s' dreamy, polite suburban living experiment gave way to long-haired, outspoken children empowered by a new era of rebellion.

I didn't want revolt as much as I wanted escape. David was the bandmate I wanted to play music with after school in the garage, losing ourselves in time and chords, far away from boring homework and tense family dinners. He was the caring older brother for whom I would have traded in my two biological ones gladly in exchange for this perfect model who'd assumed man-of-the-house reins when fictional Mr. Partridge mysteriously died, leaving the family in an economic crunch. How the dad died didn't matter to me. I was smitten with cool mom and groovy older brother running the family show.

In my experience, fathers were distracted at best and mean at worst. When my dad walked in the door after work, I gave him a wide berth and stayed in my room out of sight. From behind the closed door, I felt Pavlovian anxiety when I heard the squeaky wheels of his car pull up in the driveway and the motor make sounds like a deflating metal balloon as he turned the engine off. I'd been on the receiving end of too many harsh comments like "For God's sake, get out of my way" and silent swats as he walked in, dropped his briefcase, and headed to my parents' bedroom to change out of his suit. At dinner, his temper could rear up with the speed of a cheetah pouncing on prey. When provoked, he was prone to strike, but it wasn't the occasional physical violence that kept me wary. It was the unabated threat of it. I related—in my real and reel lives—to boys without dads. That's probably why I never bonded, as arguably so many of my peers did, with *The Brady Bunch,* another family show—albeit one with a strong, caring father—which had premiered a year before the Partridges.

Soon after we returned from Pittsburgh and *The Partridge Family* started, my family experienced seismic shifts that created a permanent sense of shakiness at home. My sister entered college and, within a year, stunned us all by getting engaged to a blond-haired, blue-eyed man who looked like a teen idol, a cross between Bobby Sherman and Shaun Cassidy, David's half-brother who became a heartthrob in his own right with his remake of the Crystals' "Da Doo Ron Ron." My brothers ran with a restless pack, occasionally leaving home for extended, mysterious periods, possibly outrunning the law. My parents were in a constant state of anxiety and aggravation. I retreated into silence, out of the way not only of diffi-cult Dad, but also of Mom, siblings, and potential bullying.

My siblings' overt rebellion—drugs, anger, getting sus-pended from school, and marrying too young—inspired my feelings of unrest and awakened furtive desires. I was egged on by *The Par-tridge Family*'s opening song, "C'mon Get Happy," which, each week, called out to me like Alice's beckoning mirror. As a curious and slightly desperate preteen, eager to escape my harsh black-and-white reality, I couldn't wait to bound into the magical color console. Leap into the television's looking glass is exactly what I did.

I found the courage to request sole occupation of our family TV room on Friday nights from eight to nine P.M., the first time I remember making such a bold appeal. Perhaps my parents decided to toss me this bone as an inexpensive way to create some peace and harmony. Or maybe they admired the quiet kid's taking a stand. I'll never know. But I got my wish and my time slot was sacrosanct.

First, I watched the Bradys' opening act, somewhat disdain-fully. Mr. Brady was nice to his blended brood of three sons and three stepdaughters, and as I watch episodes now, I'm struck by the show's dull dialogue and banal aesthetic. The Bradys weren't wry—they weren't even wry-lite. So many of their plots revolved around how best to fit in with the popular crowd. On the other side of the suburban street, the Partridges proffered an edgy colloquial spin on familial relations and purposefully set themselves apart. I loved how the cool singing kids and their hip parent procured wacky touring transportation, opting for the retro scholastic chic of an old school bus. Ordinary yellow wouldn't do, so they repainted it themselves. It was only recently that I looked closely at that bus and noticed how the Partridges painted it in a pattern derivative of Piet Mondrian, the Dutch painter instrumental in the de Stijl art movement. They avoided the psychedelic *Scooby Doo*–ish "Mystery Machine" colors, so very groovy and typical then.

After *The Brady Brunch,* I waited what seemed like an

interminable amount of time through commercial breaks until, at eight thirty P.M., the main attraction kicked off. Keith and family swooped me away in the Mondrian bus for a half hour's ride to adventures unknown, escaping into a private Valhalla I hated to leave when the credits rolled at nine P.M.

Friday night soon became my beacon, a small lighthouse offering me refuge after a week of choppy emotional seas caused by family stress and a suffocating school daze. I felt a breathless need to share air with people who actually understood me—a tribe I hadn't met yet. With temporary TV room dibs, scarfing down Coke and the mushroom pizza I was allowed to order only on Friday, I experienced a connection that felt like a state of grace. Time after time, family crisis after crisis, Keith and Shirley Partridge understood and consoled. They knew what to say and do when Chris and Tracy ran away after being scolded, or when Danny thought he was dying after a tonsillectomy, or when Laurie had a meltdown over braces.

At nine P.M., my brothers or dad usually entered the room to reclaim our one television set. I'd disappear to my bedroom and shut the door, sad that my time with Keith was over that week.

One chilly Friday fall evening during the show's second season, the year David Cassidy's popularity took off like a rocket shooting past humdrum galaxies into the outermost solar system of teen stardom, I raced upstairs from our family room. I had a three-minute commercial break from more adventures with the poster boy for millions of young girls and, now I suspect, more than a few boys. I dashed to the kitchen for a Coke refill, passing the dining room, where my sister and mother were drinking wine and talking intently. My mother had uncorked a jug bottle of Gallo Chablis, which she'd told me was slightly sour tasting but always did the trick. My father was out at a poker game. No one mentioned my brothers, about whose whereabouts we'd all stopped inquiring. There'd been no sign of them that day. Asking where they were or when they'd return home was a surefire route to stress. With the men out, it was a calmer, mostly testosterone-free zone and I felt safer. Typically, I wasted no time or words on my quick kitchen stopovers. But tonight was different. I was curious about my sister's conspiratorial whispers, which sounded dramatic, like secrets worth uncovering. I quickly deduced she was dissecting an argument she'd had with her teen-idol fiancée, while my mother confided her unhappiness with our dad. She said he was difficult to live with because he always cast a pall over family occasions. "Your father can't just have a pleasant time," she said. "He has to ruin it."

My mother smiled when I appeared and asked, "How's your show?"

"Good. It's cool," I replied quickly. "I have to get back. It's a commercial."

"Okay," she replied, her eyes slightly glazed and her smile placid but buzzed from the wine and the True menthol cigarette she was smoking.

Following an impulse I ponder to this day, my sister turned directly toward me and asked, "What is it with you and this show?"

"What?" I asked. I felt defensive about my independent Friday hour, the one time of the week I could be myself without reproach. I feared its being taken away before it felt fully mine. Was I about to be criticized?

"Do you have a crush on someone on it or something?" she asked, twirling strands of her thick, light-brown hair, which she'd probably straightened with orange juice cans earlier that evening.

"Yes," I replied, beaming what I now realize was the scared, exhilarated smile you show when someone cracks your secret code. The smile you reveal when you finally spill a secret, admit you're in love, or both. In that brief moment, beauty and truth win out over your fear about what anyone else thinks.

I turned beet red as both of them noticed my reaction and sat up a little straighter.

"Is it on a boy or a girl?" my sister asked. It was the first time anyone ever indicated that it was possible not only to have a crush on someone of the same sex but also to utter that prospect out loud.

"Boy," I replied quickly, not sure what this would mean, feeling like a determined but teetering funambulist.

My mother's expression changed ever so slightly, her curiosity piqued. But she wasn't as invested as my sister, whose eyes widened like nosy saucers.

"Really?" she asked. "Who?"

I bubbled out, "His name is David, too, and he's the coolest guy in the world. I really like him."

It wasn't a completely unguarded moment. But it was as close to one as I'd had. I was self-aware enough to hear a voice within say, "Uh-oh, you better not act too excited. Don't show too much." I knew my admission meant something, and there would be no going back.

"What does he look like?" she asked.

"He's got this really cool shag hairstyle and the whole family plays in a band and he's funny," I said. I looked at my mother, whose smile was slight and noncommittal. "But it's not too long, Mom. He's not a hippie or anything like that."

My sister gave my mom a quick, knowing look. My mother resolutely refused to raise an eyebrow. I could see the wheels in my sister's mind turn as she thought of potential follow-up questions. The possibility hung in the air for several long, pregnant seconds until I said, "I have to get back. The show's going to come back on."

I made it to the kitchen, retrieved another Coke, and sped back to my sofa seat.

After that interchange, my small-screen crush on *The Partridge Family*'s male lead was exposed. But openness wasn't a door to discussion. I was a low-key, quiet boy, not prone to spontaneous revelations, and no one asked me questions that I wondered about myself, like why I didn't feel the same intense longing for Susan Dey, who played Keith's sister Laurie. Crushes weren't a part of any conversations I had at home again. My sister was away at college and I saw her rarely. But my mother noticed my growing fascination with all things Partridge. She digested it in the context of my cousin Sandra, born three weeks after me, who was also a fan of the show and of David.

For Christmas 1970, my mother bought Sandra, who had gorgeous sandy curls and a sweet disposition, and me *The Partridge Family Album,* the group's first. The record designer made it red and textured to resemble an old-fashioned photo collection with a picture of the entire clan—and small insets of David and Shirley—on the back. It featured the group's biggest hit, "I Think I Love You," which I liked but didn't love, unlike the rest of the world, including adorable Sandra, who started dancing and singing every time she heard it. Stirred by David, too, Sandra openly expressed her simpler attraction. The adults applauded her girly beaming and girlish crush as a worthy rite of passage. After all, my mother's had been Frank Sinatra. My aunt's had been Elvis Presley. I knew I wouldn't be afforded the same entrée to this club. I was silently jealous of the freedom and tradition.

I liked that the group's most popular song didn't have the same dizzying effect on me that it had on everyone else. I felt different, superior, less shallow, not just a mere fan—someone who *paid close attention to more than the obvious.* I imagined that "I Think I Love You" wasn't David's favorite, either. In his May 1972 *Rolling Stone* interview, which I devoured along with all magazines covering him, he explicitly said that he wanted to be a rocker like Jimi Hendrix, not a bubblegum artist like Bobby Sherman. I was sure that studio executives made him sing it to appeal to the unsophisticated masses.

My favorite song on that album was "I'm on the Road," which featured the lyrics:

> *The morning whispers follow me, come my way*
> *By noon, I'm on the far side of the sun*

And I can't keep these wheels from rolling
Into one more town

There's so much to be seen and done
To settle up before I settle down

So I'm on the road
Travelin' free and easy

I wanted to go on the road with David Cassidy. Later on, I was fascinated by the beat generation. It's easy to see now that I wanted to be a smaller Neal Cassady—or perhaps a mini Allen Ginsberg—to David's grown-up Jack Kerouac. Just what unusual friendship we'd develop was as devoid of clarity, as full of spontaneity, and as deeply meaningful as what Sal Paradise and Dean Moriarty had lived through.

David Cassidy was a magic man casting spells that were powerful and confusing for a kid my age. He did not possess James Dean's brand of brooding and torture—a look and attitude I'd melt for a few years later. He brooded in his own distinct way, over teenage angsty concerns that I didn't fully understand but wanted desperately to discover, like broken hearts and high school drama. But I wasn't ready for James Dean. I needed a starter man-boy, a slowly opening gateway to the real male deal, a baby rebel with an undefined cause.

I may have been feeling a lot, but it wasn't showing. Or maybe the clueless around me just weren't tapping into the growing restlessness the show brought out in me. I was unbridled in that half hour, a boy without reins, not confined to a trotting ring, able to gallop freely. It gave my psyche a night off from the deep-rooted conventionality engulfing me like thick, heavy smoke.

When I wanted to run away from home, which was more and more frequently after my tenth birthday, my new favorite Partridge song was "Point Me in the Direction of Albuquerque"—I related to the episode in which the song was performed. In it, the family picked up a hitchhiker named Jenny who asked for a ride to Albuquerque to meet up with her father. Not knowing that they were harboring a runaway, the unsuspecting Partridges arrived en famille to find her wanted by the police. Jenny lived with her grandparents in Nebraska but ran away every other week to go to her father in Albuquerque. In between running away, she longed for her dad. This episode allowed me to flirt with the feeling of longing for a dad and wanting to do the same thing Jenny did, but that feeling passed quickly. In the end, the family left Jenny, her grandparents, and her father alone to sort their lives out, with the implication that they'd work out conflicts to everyone's satisfaction. I didn't buy it. I imagined Jenny bolting from her family to board the Piet Mondrian bus and to rejoin the Partridges as they drove off to next week's episode. I hated that she was surrounded by people yet was still so alone.

Two years into the series, I became friends with an effeminate boy my age named Steve, a school chum who was slight, blond, and looked like Earring Magic Ken pre–Barbie and puberty. When he opened his mouth, an entire display of pink Pucci purses fell out. After I spent the day at the Springfield shopping mall with Steve, my parents took me aside to tell me that there were "scary people who went by the name 'homosexual' in the world" and I had to "be careful to avoid them."

"You see," said my conservative Virginian father, clearing his throat for the fourth time before getting his caution out, Steve, the eleven-year-old potential priss-pot predator, "might try to do things to" (or worse, *with*) me, and I "should be on guard." My parents couldn't have been more uncomfortable during this conversation; I couldn't have been more defensive or closed down. I simply nodded after their awkward warning. *Teeny queens can be predators. Got it.*

I could be myself with Steve, the only person who knew the extent of my crush. I called him Friday nights after the show to review and dissect every plot point and musical number. We devoured *Teen Beat, 16,* and *Tiger Beat,* hiding the teenybopper, girly-centric magazines under our beds as if they were porn. I was intrigued by David's life and gobbled up every tidbit of information I could find. I knew that he was close to his real-life stepmother, Shirley Jones; he had a tentative relationship with his own dad and mom; he drove a white Chevrolet Corvette; and his best friend was Sam Hyman. I started drinking 7Up when I discovered it was his favorite drink and liked him even more when I found out we both loved horses. I started telling people I was "a jeans and T-shirt kind of guy" because that's what David said in an interview. I called Steve from a barbershop on the day I asked my stylist to work impossible magic and—with a wave of his comb and scissors—transform my dark curly hair into a shag style like Cassidy's. I looked in the mirror and felt a sense of victory. My mother had claimed that not eating leafy green salad would cause my hair to fall out and I'd never be able to get the Cassidy shag, and I had believed her.

After I got my faux shag—with the help of a blow-dryer wielding more horsepower than my family's Ford LTD—Steve and I attended an afternoon showing of the film *Cabaret* in Crystal City, which sounds like the place unicorns go to retire.

My sexual awakening got a Kit Kat Club–worthy charge from seeing flamboyant Liza Minnelli at her most divinely decadent strut around a seedy nightclub as she high-kicked her way in and out of relationships with closeted bisexual men. After that dirty, sexy Fosse experience, Steve and I got bolder in our assessment of David. We ripped the most seductive photos of him from teen magazines and pored over them, noting his light brown eyes, which always looked blue to me, and the compelling way he looked at the camera while leaning up against a tree; wondering what he'd look like out of the blue-and-white paisley shirt.

Begrudgingly, my parents let me continue my friendship with Steve, despite his naïve brag a week after seeing *Cabaret* that he was now the youngest member of Limelight on Liza, billed as Minnelli's "official international fan club." I suppose that admission was as close to officially coming out as anything a twelve-year-old could say in 1973. It should have clued us all in that quixotic Steve wouldn't be put off by a little parental disapproval. I always attributed his lack of filter to being raised by a lax, liberal single mother. I was raised with conservative expectations. My parents liberally offered only two things—disapproval and caution.

When *The Partridge Family* abruptly ended in 1974, David morphed into a solo artist while I became a full-fledged teen. I replaced my small-screen crush with real-time ones who remained equally unreal, stuck in the vast, silent closet inside my teenage head. Then one blessed day on the cusp of twenty, the age David was when he joined *The Partridge Family,* I landed in the right place in real time with a crush who reciprocated.

During summer break between my sophomore and junior years in college, I worked in Southern California, where I met Greg, a twenty-four-year-old actor with a short, seventies shag and brown eyes, working at Universal Studios, not far from the Warner Bros. forty-acre back lot where the Partridges filmed their show. He was the first man I'd been attracted to who was out and I made a decision after our first night together to come out. If this was what a crush felt like when it got returned and morphed into a relationship, then I wanted more. The risks seemed inconsequential compared to the reward. When we weren't together, I thought about him all the time and pined for us to spend nights together with the windows in his apartment open, feeling the cool Southern California breeze as we slept. When I headed back to my East Coast school, our summer romance didn't translate to a fall long-distance relationship.

I returned to Virginia from Los Angeles and came out, or rather started the staggered process of coming out, which took years. In chronological order, I tentatively told a couple of close friends, then a larger network of pals, my sister, my divorced parents, and the rest of my family. My mom reacted the way Shirley Partridge might have—caring and quick to make it seem okay. My dad was as irascible as ever.

"I don't care what your sexual orientation is," he said, "but I am concerned for your health," a reasonable comment given early grim news reports about AIDS. To which I replied, "Don't be. I'll be fine." After a pause, he added, "Don't expect me to ever discuss it."

A few years ago, after giving a reading in Boston for a book I'd written about gay relationships, I attended a David Cassidy concert. I read in a local alternative paper that he was appearing the one night I was in town and decided on the spur of the moment to buy a ticket. I went alone, curious about what the experience of seeing him—now in his fifties and playing the nostalgia concert circuit with groups like Herman's Hermits and the Monkees—would be like for my fortysomething self. When I walked into the concert venue, Partridge Family tunes and some of David's solo hits like "Cherish" wafted out of large speakers posted at each corner of the room. I ordered a Wild Turkey Manhattan with a 7Up chaser and leaned into the bar.

I looked around the room and saw mostly middle-aged women, dressed like soccer moms, chatting and girlishly twirling when one of the Partridge chords resonated and triggered muscle memory in their happy feet. I imagined Sandra, a soccer mom herself, at the concert with me—only now with the real me who'd openly share the exuberance she'd shown decades before.

Then the lights dimmed and he appeared, heading to the center-stage microphone with the confident lope I remembered from the show. He looked smaller than in my imagination and heavily made up, but still handsome. When he greeted the crowd with "I bet some of you remember this" and I heard the first chords of "C'mon Get Happy," I felt a jolt of electricity rock my body, a primal tremor resurrecting ancient memories from my childhood's family basement. I hadn't followed David's career for decades, but long after their popularity faded, I never lost my love for him or *The Partridge Family*. As each new generation of technology emerged, I updated my massive collection of their music from record to cassette to CD to digital. The music that had rooted me to newly discovered desires within myself still played in the background—not as often, but nonetheless it remained a low, rumbling, steady soundtrack to my life. I wistfully wondered about what had happened to both of us in the intervening years.

We all grow up and we either accept ourselves or we don't. How had we held up under the strains of time?

Since Greg, I'd been in love a few times, most recently with Vic, my partner of five years. I'd heard that David Cassidy—married for the third time, father of several children, scattershot career subsequent to *The Partridge Family*—felt bitterly stuck within the limits that being teen idol and alter ego Keith Partridge had imposed on him. But I didn't sense that in person.

While entertaining the crowd, he encouraged us to go back to our younger self and rediscover the inner gawky fan within—that impressionable youth still ineffably longing for the first perfect object of our affection. He was like Zeus coming down from Mount Olympus for a brief, rocking return engagement to acknowledge and own the unquantifiable amount of energy, hopes, and dreams long ago placed on his slim shoulders. I wondered how he was able to assimilate the heady truth that he sparked the first desires of a generation that will forever cherish him in its reveries. *How odd that must be for him,* I thought as I watched this pied piper of crushes—with his dark, dyed hair, his ever-boyish face, and a short haircut that was a far cry from his beloved shag—call forth the still-teenage souls in the room.

I watched soccer moms leave their husbands and friends and move toward the stage, demonstrate their fealty, and return to their lighter, wide-eyed, younger selves. As female fans rushed the stage, reaching up to their quinquagenarian bubblegum demigod, who was reaching back, I noticed several men my age, alone and standing on the sidelines like me. They were mouthing the words to songs like I was, slowly removing the self-conscious cloaks we'd worn into the concert venue. Ah, we were there. We are everywhere. We've been here all along.

My eye caught the glance of one of the men, who moved toward the bar where I'd encamped. He ordered a beer refill and I struck up a conversation.

"Did you ever think you'd be seeing David Cassidy live?" I asked.

"No," he laughed. "I think I'm caught in a time warp."

"I feel like my ten-year-old self just arrived and ordered a cocktail," I said, and smiled. Before David ended with—what else?—a rousing version of "I Think I Love You," he stopped singing solo midway, stuck the microphone out toward the audience, and cheered, "Now your turn!"

"Look at the crowd swarming him on the stage," he said.

"I know. I am tempted to join them," I replied.

"Were you a big Partridge Family fan?" he asked.

"Definitely," I said. "Especially Keith."

My new friend paused and said a little sheepishly, "Me too."

I laughed and recognized in his smile the scared exhilaration you show when someone cracks your secret code. The smile you reveal when you finally spill a secret, admit you're in love, or both. When, for that brief moment, beauty and truth win out over fear and concern with what anyone else thinks.

"Grab your drink, let's get a little closer to the stage," I said.

PART 6

It Had to Be You

First crushes can equal transference. Those we eventually love in real life are carbon copies of our crushes, whether we realize it at first blush or years later. Whether consciously or subconsciously, we seek out real-life loves who mirror our crush in looks, actions, or just an indefinable but unmistakable similarity.

DAVID KEPLINGER

Deborah Harry Doesn't Dance

t is 1979 and I am in the seventh grade and I am watching *American Bandstand,* where, center stage, Deborah Harry stands behind her stiff steel microphone, slightly smiling, singing. It is the song I heard at the Skate Ranch on Route 309, a driving "One Way or Another," and she is like all the girls I loved then and all the girls I will love and there's something else: she doesn't really look at the camera; she doesn't really look at the microphone. Her eyes are just rising a little ways behind me to a place about four feet off the floor. Wherever I am watching her from, that spot is just behind me. Which leaves me, twelve years old and five feet tall, hair "feathered back" (as my mother would describe to the beautician), feeling decidedly unsuitable, like I should look back over my shoulder at the lucky guy who is.

Deborah Harry doesn't dance. She might throw a red scarf around like a giant, ridiculous handkerchief. But no dancing. The scarf accentuates the fact. She is teasing as she reprimands. Then she throws the scarf over her shoulder again.

I see her now, thirty-seven years later, in videos from that period, old television spots that appear on YouTube. This *Bandstand* episode is one of them. In this one, her boys in skinny ties strum Gibson guitars or bang at the drums. Her post-punk/pre–New Wave raunch kind of flaunts the fact that this is as far as it's going to go, boys and girls; you will float here in this blue-ball hell, it says to me; you will live in this light between fighting and fucking. It's excruciating. It's exhilarating to be between so much, such joy and frustration, anger and ecstasy. It is a feeling I would have described then as "good." That's how it was in 1979. It felt good to watch Deborah Harry on *American Bandstand*. To be her five-foot-tall voyeur. To stand just a little in front of the real guy she's looking at. I watch the video on my computer. And I feel it all roiling in my gut again. Only now do I see her largesse and intelligence and the sculpted cheekbones, the unblinking eyes, the nearly emotionless challenge—*feel good?*—rising out of her expression. Only now do I see how beautiful she was then. She won't dance for you. She is herself.

Only now do I see it: the look that Charlize Theron, to name just one of her emanations, has drawn from Deborah Harry's early glamour. In the *Bandstand* appearance Deborah Harry could be Theron's twin. Only now do I see how those subtle turns of the hip, that resistance to actually dancing, that I-won't-dance-don't-ask-me kind of dance, is sexier and more suggestive than the real thing. There's something *reasonable* about it. There will be no fighting, there will be no fucking, but I understand that if there must be something, her movements say, there will be this.

So it happens all over again. It is 1979 and I am in the seventh grade and I am watching *American Bandstand,* where on the wide stage Deborah Harry stands in a gold miniskirt with yellow stockings on, and she is taking the microphone out of the socket, and she is doing a little circle around the metal pole saying: *I'm gonna meetcha meetcha meetcha meetcha.* The guitars never blare into the squealing solo. But there is the option, the promise, always. There is the possibility. Everything is possibility. It is 1979 and I am in the seventh grade and Deborah Harry wears her new short hair like Elizabeth, whose parents are from Hungary, and whom I say hello to at the seventh-grade Get to Know Ya Party. The girls are sitting on one side of the gymnasium. The boys are sitting on the other side of the gymnasium. The boys are always jumping on top of each other, trying to make the other one flinch. I always flinch. Elizabeth is looking at someone just behind me. The boys are on the verge of fighting. The girls are laughing and watching one another. Everyone—and here is the wonderful thing—is in love with someone in that room. Blondie on the radio. Nobody, nobody dances.

ANNA BRESLAW

Jarlsberg and Sourdough

In 1999, when I was twelve years old, I saw *Drive Me Crazy* in theaters with a bunch of other girls from my class for a birthday celebration, and I fell hard for Adrian Grenier (not yet famous for playing Vincent Chase in *Entourage*).

He played an antiestablishment rebel, and he and the popular girl next door mutually fall for each other. His mom died of cancer but he doesn't make a big deal of it and is therefore fully unaware that such *#tragedies* are majorly appealing to girls. And he happened to look like Earth's closest approximation to a Disney prince. By the time we left the theater, my feelings were beyond the frivolous "gush about him with the other girls" level. This was a sulky-only-silent-girl-at-the-sleepover-because-what-are-these-hormones-I'm-feeling kind of crush.

After casually suggesting my family rent *The Adventures of Sebastian Cole* at Blockbuster "for no reason," I did have a dim awareness of what about him appealed to me. He was low-key, chillaxed, and various other adjectives for "stoned" (which, of course, I didn't even fully understand at the time). He never seemed like he was trying too hard or was too concerned about anything. Being from a family of Olympic worriers myself, I found this appealing.

Leonardo DiCaprio, the A-list hottie of the time, was anything but casual. He was pretty and boyish—fey, almost—and wanted to be a *Serious Actor*. You got the feeling he'd make a "no punching above the shoulders" rule if he got in a fight. Nothing about him *scared* me. Grenier was one step ahead of DiCaprio on the masculine evolutionary scale, an intoxicating juxtaposition of pretty and *guy*-ish, the kind of guy who had a messy room and played bass and only realized he was handsome when a high volume of girls started coming up to him at parties and saying things like, "You're soooo random." He was accessible in a way that grown-up male heartthrobs were not, but he scared me in a way that prepackaged tween dreamboats didn't. All of which is to say, he was sexy, and I *could not even*.

I shared a room with my sister, and we didn't have our own stereo system, so I'd hijack the entire living room to lie on the couch like a psychiatrist's patient in a *New Yorker* cartoon and listen to Sarah McLachlan's *Mirrorball*.

One particular line in "Building a Mystery"—a line that seemed to have struck many adolescent girls now in their late twenties, judging by how gleefully and ironically my friends and I scream it when it comes on at a bar—made me think of Grenier, or at least his characters: *You're a beautiful, a beautiful fucked-up man.* I sometimes wrote the line in cursive over numerous photos I traced of him in my sketchbook, printed at the school library. I'd sometimes freedraw them. (This was also deep in my anime period.)

I didn't realize how embarrassing this would all be to put in a book. Oops!

As I entered high school, Grenier's roles remained that one short step ahead of me, out of reach but just barely, symbolic of the elusive "older guy." *Entourage*'s first season was my junior year of high school, and it solidified what I'd always secretly crushed on him for: he was hot, but he didn't really *care* that he was hot. He was just a dude who liked hanging out with his friends. Bros before hos!

Adorable! At the same time, I felt a little jealous, in a hipster way: I'd seen the passive nothingness in him first! I was well into the age when most girls were transitioning from screen crushes to the more attainable variety, but the only guys I ever liked always had Grenier-esque elements (the popular guy who didn't seem to care about being popular and secretly wanted to be an artist; the quiet guy from an infamously messed-up family) and were almost as out of my league as the hottie himself.

Like most girls my age with a celebrity crush that intense, I felt simultaneously ahead of the pack—for having such good taste and being unwilling to settle—and behind it: when Erica Ross asked at a sophomore-year slumber party who had "given head," I had no idea what it meant but immediately raised my hand just to avoid being left out, and I was the only one who did.

By college, I'd mostly outgrown him, although I'd always fall back to a storm of Google searches whenever he popped up on-screen. Like when I saw *The Devil Wears Prada* and he played Anne Hathaway's live-in boyfriend: he has a handful of unimportant scenes that largely consist of his making her dinner and whining about how she's obsessed with her job and is never home anymore. When I distilled my crush on Grenier down to its essence, it was this: he looked like a frat boy and a high-fashion model ran really fast into each other, but he seemed totally cool with falling back and letting other people—including women—be in charge.

Today, I Am a Woman. But Adrian Grenier remains, frozen in time, as an older guy. When I think about dating him now, I imagine the smell of stale weed, the clanking of a toxin-free water canteen clipped to his belt with an unnecessary number of carabiners, as if he's in the Mojave Desert rather than downtown Los Angeles. I imagine sitting through dull and incessant conversations about the virtues of sustainable living. Trying not to wince at the latest news article about him on Google, whose headline reads: "Adrian Grenier: 'We'll have to pay for it when the oceans collapse.'" Less a daydream, more of a nightmare.

I think my crush on him always was, at its core, because he is exactly what a *New York Times* film critic might call "bland and passive." But that's just the most negative interpretation of *my* crush. He could also be considered a calm, supportive guy who happens to be unfathomably attractive but still down-to-earth, secure enough in his masculinity to let the people around him call the shots, who's willing to make his girlfriend a Jarlsberg-and-sourdough grilled cheese—without making a huge deal about What An Awesome Boyfriend He Is—when she gets home from her job at a women's magazine. I guess I should thank Adrian Grenier for providing a nearly dead-on blueprint of my happy adulthood. Or his agent, since he probably didn't make any of those decisions himself. God love him.

YESHA CALLAHAN

My Own Private Danny Zuko

rowing up in New Jersey during the eighties, you could always count on Saturday afternoon movies to keep the boredom at bay. And if you weren't one of the fortunate ones to have cable television, you were pretty much limited to a handful of TV channels. But in my single-television house, trying to get to watch what you wanted with three other siblings around was always a fight to the finish. It was basically first come, first served, or who could rip the remote control out of someone's hand the fastest. And I'm quite sure my sister still remembers the headlock she got put in on one particular rainy Saturday morning during our daily fight for the remote control.

That day, when I was nine years old, I found myself flipping through the channels while listening to my siblings argue in the background. It was a toss-up between kung fu on channel 5 and kung fu on channel 11. For some reason kung fu Saturdays were a big thing in the eighties on television. As I was flipping through the channels, something caught my eye. At first I flipped past, but then I went back. I don't even know why I did, but for the next ninety minutes, I was mesmerized. Here was this boy named Tod Lubitch. I'd never seen the actor playing him before in my life. But I was immediately mesmerized. The thick hair. The grayish-blue eyes. And that dimple in his chin. It wasn't long before I asked my mother about *The Boy in the Plastic Bubble*.

"Honey, that's John Travolta. He grew up not too far from here," I remember her replying.

Travolta.

Yesha Travolta.

It kind of had a cool ring to it.

And that's when it happened. I immediately became obsessed. While other kids my age were immersed in things like Nickelodeon, I was immersed in everything Travolta.

Besides thinking that Travolta was the best thing since roller skates, I related to his character in the movie. No, I didn't live in a bubble, but sometimes I felt like life would have been easier that way. Unlike Lubitch, I wasn't someone who couldn't go outside because he'd die, but I was that kid who was allergic to everything. My best friend was an EpiPen, a handheld needle that I stuck into my thigh whenever I felt a twinge of allergen trouble. That EpiPen went wherever I went. To even start to count the number of things I was allergic to as a kid would probably take at least thirty minutes. But to narrow it down, let's just say pollen and grass were not my friends and neither were fresh fruits like apples, peaches, pears, watermelon, or plums. A plastic bubble would have done me a lot of good back then, especially when it came to going outside and playing with other kids in the spring.

And then there were those people who immediately felt sorry for me. Lubitch had his Gina Biggs in the movie, the woman who fell in love with him despite his bubble. Well, I didn't have a Gina; I just had people who were always making sure I wasn't around anything I was allergic to. Yeah, a bubble would have been nice back then.

Travolta's character in *The Boy in the Plastic Bubble* had me hooked on everything Travolta. Sure it was odd for a nine-year-old, but no one questioned it.

At last count, I've watched *Saturday Night Fever* eighty-seven times. *Grease* forty-three times. *Urban Cowboy* twenty-one times. And *Pulp Fiction* over one hundred times. Sure, some of Travolta's movies were pure trash. Seriously, how many people actually watched *Battlefield Earth*? Even with the crappy movies, Travolta was still my first crush.

Tall. Dark hair and those eyes. And I can't forget the rhythm. You cannot deny the fact that Travolta had moves back then.

I'm pretty sure I was probably the only girl my age with a crush on Travolta. Especially being a black girl. But I was always taught by my parents that things like skin color didn't matter one bit. There was no one around to tell me that I shouldn't be lusting after a white guy. Until I actually started to.

Growing up in a neighborhood in New Jersey that was highly Italian wasn't that easy as a teenager. I remember one hot summer in 1989, my Italian neighbors were in their pool and my siblings and I were sitting outside on the porch looking over at them having fun. One of the neighbor's relatives looked over the fence and yelled, "Look at the little porch monkeys." OMG—horrific. At the time I was thirteen years old, and although I had never heard that name before, I knew it wasn't anything nice. I immediately ran into the house and told my mother. She quickly ran back outside and grabbed my siblings, and yelled a few curse words at the neighbors.

"Don't ever look over their way again," my mother yelled.

And I didn't. Until a few weeks later when my neighbor's grandson came to visit for the summer.

Enzo was fifteen years old and taller than the average kid his age. He had jet-black hair and crystal-gray eyes that changed to blue at times. He was my very own John Travolta. If "swagger" were a term used back then, he would have been full of it. Every time I heard Enzo outside bouncing his basketball I ran outside to sit on my porch. I knew my mother had warned us not to look over to their house anymore, but I couldn't help it. Enzo reminded me so much of Travolta it was ridiculous.

Should I say something to him? Should I wait for him to say something to me? What if he was like his family member who called us porch monkeys? I knew I would regret it if I didn't say anything, but I also didn't want my feelings hurt.

One day I finally mustered up the courage.

Enzo was outside bouncing his basketball. I came outside, took a deep breath, and walked over to him. As I got closer, my heart started racing. When he looked up at me, I thought I was going to faint. Then he threw me the ball.

"Can you dribble?" he asked me.

"Of course I can dribble," I replied.

Slowly but surely, I started to dribble the basketball. Slowly but surely, my heart stopped racing. For the next two hours Enzo and I dribbled and talked. Talked and dribbled. We eventually made our way back to my porch and started talking about some of our favorite movies.

And as luck would have it, we had a crappy Travolta movie in common: *Look Who's Talking*. Enzo wasn't into *Grease* or *The Boy in the Plastic Bubble*, but that was okay. Enzo knew a lot more about Travolta than I did, especially when it came to Scientology. Although he didn't know much about the religion himself, he explained that he once overheard his parents talking about it, and all he knew was that it was weird. He knew everything from Xenu to thetans. Apparently he got interested in it because it seemed like something from *The Twilight Zone*. I couldn't believe that there was actually a religion based on something straight out of a sci-fi movie.

When I told Enzo about my crush on Travolta, he reminded me that he was in fact an old man now, compared to us.

"You do realize he's old enough to be your father?" Enzo asked.

"When you put it that way, you make it sound so disgusting," I replied.

That summer he would never let me live my crush on

Travolta down. It was prime joke material for him. But god forbid I made fun of his crush on Paula Abdul. Let him tell it, it was okay for a younger guy to crush on an older woman.

For the next couple of weeks, Enzo and I hung out practically every day. His nickname for me was Sandy, after Olivia Newton-John's character in *Grease,* of course. And I teased him by calling him Danny Zuko.

We were inseparable, until they separated us.

It was the same person who called my sisters and me porch monkeys—Enzo's uncle. One afternoon while we were outside sitting on the sidewalk, Enzo's uncle Tommy pulled up in his car. As he got out of the car, he yelled for Enzo to come over to him.

"I'll be right back, let me go and see what he wants," Enzo said.

I simply said, "Okay."

As they made their way into the house, a weird feeling overcame me. I knew exactly what was going on behind the closed door. Enzo was being told to stay away from me. And I knew exactly why.

The next day I heard Enzo outside bouncing his basketball. Usually he would come over and knock on my door, but that day he didn't. I looked outside and didn't notice his uncle's car, so I rushed out to see what he was up to.

As I reached him, he told me that he'd meet me around the corner at the park in fifteen minutes. He walked away and didn't say anything else to me. I saw him enter his house, so I made my way to the park. I sat on the swing and waited. I didn't have a watch on, so I was only estimating in my head how long fifteen minutes was. Eventually I saw him walking down the hill. I immediately jumped off the swing and met him halfway.

The look on his face. I knew he didn't have anything good to tell me. I knew my heart was about to be broken. I knew my personal John Travolta was going to tell me he couldn't be friends with me anymore.

"You know, my uncle is a jerk," Enzo said.

"Yeah, I know," I replied.

Enzo moved closer to me and my heart rate started rising. As he got closer, I felt my palms getting sweaty. Sweaty palms and a racing heart. I was a quintessential hot mess. If life were a movie, at that moment, "You're the One That I Want" would have been playing in the background.

And that's when Danny Zuko, I mean Enzo, kissed me.

It was everything I thought it would be. For weeks I'd imagined what it would be like. For weeks I'd hoped it would happen, and when it finally did, I couldn't help but giggle as his lips touched mine. That moment was perfect. I didn't want it to end. But I knew it had to and it probably would never happen again.

When we finally pulled ourselves apart, Enzo told me his uncle said he wasn't allowed to hang out with me anymore. My bottom lip immediately started to tremble and I knew what was going to happen. Soon a tear streamed down my face. Followed by more tears. I lowered my head because I felt embarrassed that I was crying in front of him. Enzo lifted my face and kissed my cheek.

"You know, there's always a way around things," Enzo said.

I wanted to believe him, but I didn't. I knew how this story was going to end. I'd had my first kiss and it was perfect, but I knew I'd never kiss Enzo again after we left the park.

We stayed in the park for hours that night, talking and laughing. I tried not to think about what was going to transpire once we left. I wanted to cherish the moment. As a teenager, I knew he would be one of many crushes. But he was my John Travolta.

After that night, I barely ever heard Enzo outside bouncing his basketball and when I did, I just peeped at him from the window. His uncle had made it clear he wasn't allowed to talk to me. The night before Enzo was to head back home, there was a knock on my door. My mother answered and told me someone was waiting for me outside.

I knew exactly who it was.

"I wanted to give these to you before I left," Enzo said as he handed me a letter and his basketball.

He then gave me a little kiss on the cheek and walked away.

As I walked back into the house with tears forming, I ran to my room and ripped open the letter.

> *Dear Yesha,*
> *You will always be my Sandy. And I'll always be your Zuko.*
>
> > *xoxo,*
> > *Enzo*

When I look back on the experience, I didn't realize until I got older just how much pressure from family members and friends can play into interpersonal relationships. That summer was ruined because of Enzo's uncle. As much as I wanted a Danny-and-Sandy ending, it didn't happen.

After that summer, we kept in touch as much as two teenagers who lived states apart could. We wrote each other and talked on the phone. But eventually we grew apart. Every once in a while, I head to Facebook to see if I can find Enzo. But to no avail. He's one of the few people in the world who doesn't have a Facebook account or a footprint on the Internet.

As a kid, having a crush on John Travolta wasn't something I thought was a big deal. But in a world that wasn't so "postracial," being a black girl and crushing on Enzo proved to be one of the hardest life lessons I had the unfortunate pleasure of learning. We were kids, and Enzo did what his uncle told him to do. He wasn't Danny. And I definitely wasn't Sandy. If I looked like Sandy, I'm quite sure the story would have had a different ending. Life isn't the plot of *Grease*. You easily can change your hair and clothes, go from greaser to bobby-soxer, but changing your family's prejudices? No amount of teenage wishes can unharden a heart.

After all of these years, I still have that letter Enzo gave me. I still have those memories. And I still have a big-ass crush on John Travolta. When I see Travolta on television now, I don't see the Travolta that people look at oddly because of his Scientology affiliation. I see Lubitch and Zuko. And most important, I see Enzo, and it brings back the memories of the summer of 1989.

Jerrys and Greggs

Though the closest I've ever come to sleeping with a celebrity was an exhausting interlude with the late poet Peter Orlovsky (best known as Allen Ginsberg's boyfriend; indeed, coition occurred in Ginsberg's apartment), my failure to become a rock-and-roll groupie in the seventies and eighties reflects only a lack of opportunity. Having no clue as to how one would go about gaining entrée backstage or to a hotel suite, wishful thinking took over. The men I loved, whether for a night or for years or in one suppressed moan of appreciation, often looked like stunt doubles of rock stars. My twin passions for the Grateful Dead and the Allman Brothers were reflected in my two major types: Jerry Garcias and Gregg Allmans.

Jerry's hair made him an easy doppelgänger for boys with Jew-fros—add the wire-rims and a bit of facial hair, put on "Uncle John's Band," and you've got a magical night of romance. Along with the coiffure, these young men often had something more—the brooding, sensitive, playful, drug-soaked spirit one could just sense emanating from Jerry. Several also knew the chords to "Sugar Magnolia" and "Friend of the Devil." I had not one, not two, but three serious boyfriends in the Garcia mold, each creating subtypes of his own—High School Jerry (we lost our virginities together), Big Tall Drink of Jerry, and Jerry in the Mental Hospital.

Greggs were a different story. They too were defined by their hair—in this case, super long, straight and shiny, preferably blond—but unlike those menschy Jerrys, a Gregg revealed himself after one shampoo-commercial night of love to be a redneck, a sexist, or some other kind of creep. One stole my guitar, one pissed in my tent at a music festival, one was a guy who had been an undergraduate at my college for at least eight years. He may still be there today, picking up freshmen, these days perceived as a graying Jared Leto. And as for Peter Orlovsky—it was the ponytail, not the poetry. He was a middle-aged, Slavic, bisexual Gregg.

My sister went for Mick Jaggers, characterized by their big, luscious lips and their womanizer personalities. My best friend never found a good Neil Young but she did have a dream that Neil Young gave her a puppy. My first husband, a gay guy from Philadelphia, was a bit of a Daryl Hall. He was going out with a little Italian John Oates before we met. In my love-struck gaze, he was nothing but a David Bowie.

Once upon a time, girls wanted to sleep with Rod Stewart or Keith Richards; I for some reason just wanted their hairdos. I used to bring album covers to the salon and say, This. Just like this.

A couple years ago, I was trading stories with a bunch of women at the Woodstock Writers Festival. In Woodstock, they get the real thing. One gal had slept with the actual Jerry Garcia (!!), another was Sterling Morrison's widow, and a third still had something going with Chris Isaak. Or maybe it was Chris Cross. One of the two.

"Well, I slept with Lou Reed," a gal I'll call Marie put in.

Lou Reed, we sighed.

It was ages ago, she explained, in Minneapolis, where one of her best friends was a nearly professional groupie. She had already notched Robert Plant, Barry White, and two members of J. Geils, but was still working to hook up with their hometown boy, Prince. One particular night, she was determined to make it happen, and she wanted Marie there to testify. After primping for hours, the two click-clacked into the bar where he was known to hang out.

They paused at the door to scan the crowd. Kaboom, there he was. The Artist himself. "Can you believe this luck?" Marie's friend said. Then she pointed to the bar. "And look—that's Lou Reed!"

"Which one?" Marie had heard the name, of course, but didn't know much more.

"Come on, you don't know Lou Reed when you see him? Right there, with the curly black hair."

When in Rome, figured Marie, and sidled over to Lou as her friend made a beeline for Prince. "He bought me a drink right away," she said, "and he was so much nicer than I thought he would be. So easy to talk to. And so modest."

Many drinks later, she accompanied Lou Reed back to his hotel room. Clearly he was a guy who didn't make a big deal out of being a rock star since he was staying at the Best Western, and the room wasn't trashed at all.

As it turned out, Lou Reed was an amazing lover.

In the morning, Lou told Marie he'd love to see her again next time he was in town and handed her his card. Which said, "Joe Johnson, Western Sales Manager, John Deere Inc."

"Well, if you didn't know what he looked like," Marie explained to us, "Lou Reed could easily have been an African American name, right? Like Lou Rawls."

If Jerry Garcia could be a fifteen-year-old kid from Hebrew school, why not.

JILL KARGMAN

You're the One That I Want

A hickey from Kenickie is like a Hallmark card." I didn't quite know what that meant when I first saw *Grease* as a child. I think of Hallmark cards as lame and cheesy, but subsequently learned that in the 1950s they were considered *really* special. And the famed greaser sidekick adds, "When you care enough to send the very best." Love bites have never quite been my thing, but Kenickie? I loved him so much he could have vampired me to death. But for the adoring lash-batting masses, it was Kenickie's best friend, Danny Zuko, the star, who seemed to be the one every girl swooned over.

But I have never been every girl.

When everyone loved Ferris, I fell for tragic Cameron. When hordes screamed for the throaty front man at the rock concert, I ogled the hot bassist. Again and again, my "type" is that I have no type, other than that he is always the one overshadowed by his glowier wingman, the supernova who made the other girls faint. But not me. Fuck the starlight—it's the night sky that makes them pop anyhow. The darker sidelined characters always revved my engine louder.

When *Grease* hit theaters around the world, its prized headliner was sealed in as a heartthrob. My father called him "John Revolting." While other girls wrung their Calvins over Zuko, I literally chundered at the thought—he was Puke-o to me. Even when it was nostalgia-cool to dig him during his *Pulp Fiction* renaissance when the brilliant Tarantino fished him out of the career shitter and christened him Vincent Vega avec Royale with Cheese, I loved the familiarity and kitsch value but could've hurled at the thought of fucking him. I mean, ew.

Not because of Scientology or lupine features, but because of the ghost of Zuko past. This is a guy who was such a pussified ass-face that he ditched sweet Sandy (who played serious tonsil hockey with him in the waves that summer) when his pals ridiculed his enthusiastic greeting. He had to say, "That's my name, don't wear it out!" prompting shrill Aussie shrieks of "YOU'RE NOT THE DANNY ZUKO I MET AT THE BEACH!" Yeah, well, fuck him. And that Goody Two-shoes with her dumb chucked pom-poms. They both sucked, if you asked me. And what a lame lesson their so-called love proved: change yourself completely and then the other person will like you!

I myself have always been more of a Rizzo type of girl. In fact, I played her in my high school musical senior year. Screw blond, pretty, and perfect; I much more identified with the tough cookie. Not that I was banging in backseats or planning to Dyson out a fetus if I ever got knocked up, but that somehow seemed edgier than some cheerleading blonde with *Dumb and Dumber* bangs. And why did I feel this way? Because the knocker-upper, the bad boy with the heart of gold, the stud who put the sizzling grease in "Greased Lightnin'," was my very first heartthrob: Kenickie.

It's still unclear what kind of a fucking name that is. I've yet to hear of another before or since. But that guy slayed me. They sang, "The chicks'll cream," and while I was too young to "cream" (vom, BTdubs), I do remember, as a small child of six or seven, being turned on by him. I know! Paging Dr. Freud. I look at my young daughters and swear they don't get aroused by movie stars, but who the fuck knows. It's not like I broadcasted it. I think my mom just thought I really dug the music.

I opened my vinyl album cover and would stare at him for

hours. I watched the movie on our *spanking new* VHS player and wore that tape into the ground. He was beautiful. He was flawed. He was everything. *Pourquoi?*

Some answers: First of all, he was drawn to the strong woman. He didn't care that Riz was a bit of a ballbuster. She made pronouncements, spoke her mind, and wasn't afraid to ruffle feathers. In order to protect herself, she plays it cool when she thinks she has a bun in the oven. When "good news travels fast" at the drive-in, Kenickie says he doesn't run away from his mistakes, lending instant support and a hand on her shoulder. Jeff Conaway, the actor who played my beloved, looks positively crushed when Stockard Channing coolly replies, "It's someone else's mistake." You can almost see the hurt conjuring up a mist of tears in his eyes as he looks away and says, "Thanks a lot, kid." The chink in his leather armor melted me.

For her own emotional shield, Rizzo takes up with Kenickie's pockmarked white-trash-tastic rival, who somehow has procured a vehicle with actual flames shooting out of his tailpipes. Humiliated, Kenickie sadly follows suit by escorting the at-least-twenty-nine-year-old Cha Cha DiGregorio to their high school prom. But it's all an empty gesture meant to balance the scales of infidelity— Kenickie watches, forlorn, as crater-cheeks holds his sassy vixen in red. Social-climbing and whorish Cha Cha ditches him anyway, scoring the dance prize with Zuko, who once again eclipses his hotter, cooler, sexier pal.

So smitten was I by Conaway's Kenickie, I used to tiptoe into my parents' living room in the dark (which was a big deal for me) to borrow/steal an antique magnifying glass my father had bought. It had an ivory handle and rested on a mahogany table. The poor dead-elephant tusk, warped crystal, and I would pore over the group photos of faux-yearbook collages inside the album cover and find Kenickie. Sigh . . .

When Riz finally sheds her uterine lining and has a most

welcome flag of Japan in her panties, she runs into his arms, elatedly declaring a false alarm. They embrace beneath the Ferris wheel midcarnival.

In my opinion, it is the kiss of the movie. Fuck the leather-pants-wearing and cigarette-smoking poseur Sandy or newly christened jock Zuko in his varsity letterman sweater—they each changed who they were to land the other, like a sick twisted version of "The Gift of the Magi," where it wasn't about generosity but as-similation and subversion of identity. Lame. Kenickie loved Rizzo in all her adventurous, shimmy-down-the-drainpipe glory! That cunt Patty Simcox may have gossiped about his girl, but Kenickie didn't give a shit about those preened, ponytailed student-council sock-hop-boppers. Sandy had to get a total makeover from that train wreck Frenchie to land her man. Rizzo was just herself.

But back to her paramour, Kenix.

My best friend Vanessa's fabulous late mother, Nancy, mem-orably advised us one night on her Martha's Vineyard porch: *Like the guys who like you*. She didn't understand the concept of chasing down some playboy, some project to work on, a man to morph. *Like the guys who like you*. Perhaps because I identified with Riz long before I played her, I liked the one who selected her—not because she put out, but because she was fierce. She was all woman. Opin-ionated, silly, sexy, badass. How hot is it to find a guy who's drawn to that rather than poodle skirts? I'm not ragging on Sandy because she never had a drink or pierced ears or a dick in her; I think she sucked because she was a one-way ticket to Snoozeville! Riz was never boring—she was the life of the slumber party, after all. And Kenickie saw that sparkle and it electrified him. It made him ner-vous and it made him feel things. Not just in his denim. He was exuberant when smitten, decimated when heartbroken. Lower lows but higher highs. He was in touch with his emotions, which was wildly sexy. I wanted someone just like him—that alluring mélange of a velvet fist in an iron glove. The most intoxicating combination.

Now, granted, his gum chewing and prom outfit left a lot to be desired, but in the purity of his default uniform—jeans, a black tee, a necklace that I found scaldingly hot, and his T-bird leather motorcycle jacket—he made me weak. Every viewing through the decades.

After thirty-plus years of viewing this movie, I can honestly say the guy still drives me crazy. Tastes shift, one's own romantic history colors idols or taints types, but Kenickie could still give me a hickey anytime. When I heard Jeff Conaway died in 2011, I was sad the way anyone is when a beloved actor is lost to the world. But what I also buried was a piece of my childhood, in that not only my first crush but also my huge-hearted youth was gone. Adults don't get starry eyes the way young people do. He was the closest thing to a matinee idol for me, but what he did was serve as the first spotlight on my affection for the guy in the wings. The beginning of a personal trend not to seek the star. Not the center of attention but the "lieutenant" (as he calls Danny, who takes over for him at Thunder Road and saves the day when Kenickie suffers unfortunate head trauma).

Maybe it's because I knew I could never get the "main guy" so I was drawn to the sidekick, but I think the pack often defines the leader; Danny wanted to impress Kenickie when fawning over Sandy. Steely Riz choked back tears for him. And in the end, it was their smooch that made my heart skip a beat. As for me, I've never gone for the leading stud in my own life. Only the quirky one stage left. We go together like rama-lama-lama-kadingidadingdadong. Because those guys always have so much more lightning inside them.

PART 7

So Wrong but So Right

Occasionally, we just can't figure out what about a person sparked us so. Was he or she years older, a far cry from conventionally beautiful, a cartoon or video game character, or just a downright strange object of your intense passion? As several of our contributors discovered, inappropriate crushes sometimes have more potency than puppy love.

RICHARD McCANN

The Lonely Life

We movie stars all end up by ourselves. Who knows?
Maybe we want to. —BETTE DAVIS

I n those long, mute nights following my father's sudden death, when I was eleven, I often sat with my mother in the living room of our small suburban ranch house, watching old movies on our DuMont TV. We both loved movie stars, especially those who'd been popular when my mother was still young—Joan Crawford, for instance, and Ingrid Bergman, Loretta Young, Merle Oberon, Joan Fontaine, Susan Hayward, and Gene Tierney, who had what my mother described as "Spanish eyes," just like her own, and that, she said, explained why so many of the ladies she called upon—she was the Welcome Wagon hostess of our subdivision just north of Washington, DC—always told her that she and Gene Tierney were look-alikes.

Those nights to me were special nights, just me and my mother together, and no father to scrutinize and remark upon what he had termed my "girlishness," as when he'd caught me playing school or skipping rope with some of the neighbor girls. On these nights, even though my mother disapproved of the watching of TV, she'd put down whatever thick paperback she was then reading— *Marjorie Morningstar,* perhaps, or *A Tree Grows in Brooklyn*—to tell me which of the clothes the stars were wearing were almost identical to those she had also once worn, back in the thirties or forties. Sometimes, as she smoked her endless Parliaments, stubbing out the lipstick-stained butts in a crystal ashtray, she told me about her own personal experiences with movie stars, such as Fred Mac-Murray, who'd once winked at her as they passed on the sidewalk of Sixth Avenue in New York City, or about the time she'd ridden in an elevator with Frank Sinatra in Rockefeller Center, when she was working there as a receptionist for American Petroleum.

Other nights, when she was lonely and scared and angry, as she often was in those early years of her widowhood, she'd deride almost everything—me, our little house, our dull neighbors—including even the movie stars she said she adored, as if they had somehow suddenly chagrined or failed her. She said, for instance, that Judy Garland was a drunk and a drug addict, which is why she wore three-quarter-sleeve jackets on her weekly TV show, to hide the needle marks. She said that John Garfield was really a Jew and that she could prove it because she knew his actual name, Jacob Julius Garfinkle, which was given him when he was born on the Lower East Side. Once, when I told her that I thought Barbara Stanwyck was a great actress in *Stella Dallas,* which I'd just recently watched by myself on *Million Dollar Movie,* she said that everyone knew that Barbara Stanwyck was really nothing more than "a poor man's Bette Davis," as she put it.

Among all the stars, in fact, there was only one whom she considered so great as to be beyond even the smallest reproach: that was Bette Davis herself, "the First Lady of the American Screen," at once so powerful, strong willed, and magnificent. Together, and largely in silence, like the mournful, invalided congregants one could see each Sunday morning on *Mass for Shut-Ins,* we watched *Of Human Bondage, The Petrified Forest, Marked Woman, Dark Victory,* and *The Private Lives of Elizabeth and Essex;* we watched *The Letter, The Little Foxes, Mr. Skeffington, Watch on the Rhine,* and *Phone Call from a Stranger.* Almost fifty then, and anxious that she would never meet a man again, my mother cried as we watched *Mr. Skeffington,* in which Bette Davis plays a beautiful, vain, and superficial woman—an aging flirt, neglectful of both her loyal husband and her daughter—who eventually catches diphtheria, which ravages her face. As for me, I pictured myself as Bette Davis in *Dark Victory,* in which she plays a hedonistic socialite who, in the end, becomes ennobled by going blind as she kneels in her well-kept garden one afternoon, planting hyacinths.

It was at this point that my life turned inward—it was then, that is, that my dream life became my real life, and deep within, even though I knew at least in some small way that I was playing a kind of make-pretend, I began to feel different from the boy I appeared to be to others: a pudgy, pleasant boy, praised for his manners and his Catholic piety; an anxious swain, escorting his mother to dinner at the Hot Shoppes and then accepting money from her under the table in order to pay the check, now that I was what my mother called "the man of the house." The more I watched Bette Davis—in *Juarez,* for instance, as the Empress Carlota, going mad during a confrontation with Napoleon III, as played by Claude Rains, or in *The Letter,* striding in fierce resolve at night across the porch of her and her husband's bungalow on a rubber plantation in British Malaya, as she fires shot after shot into the body of her secret lover, whom she has summoned to call on her when she is alone—the more I became like Bette Davis herself, and, as her, I somehow managed to walk with a bit less fear as I went down the junior high school corridors, where the hoods and the louts were always loitering, waiting to whisper words like "flit" and "faggot" and "cocksucker," as the younger, timid boys, like me, passed by. As her, I could even sometimes walk into the school cafeteria, looking fruitlessly for a table where I might be allowed to sit and eat my dry sandwich. Deep within, I could imagine I possessed the great, hard dignity of Elizabeth I, as Bette Davis played her in *The Virgin Queen,* and I possessed as well Elizabeth's power to calculate and execute a hideous revenge against anyone who crossed her. In fact, however, I was a widow's son who stayed at home, courteous and flattering, angry and friendless, as my mother's compensation for the missing man of the house. But I wanted what I considered then a woman's power—the power to stop a heart with a threatening glance or a sudden, stiff, and stabbing remark.

Is it any wonder, then, that as soon as I saw Bette Davis's 1962 autobiography, *The Lonely Life,* in a bookstore at our local mall, I shoplifted it, tucking it under my London Fog waterproof jacket? Or that I went back not too long after to shoplift also *The Films of Bette Davis,* a compendium of all of Davis's movies up to the most recent, *What Ever Happened to Baby Jane?,* complete with plot summaries, cast lists, critical responses, and more than two hundred black-and-white photo stills of Bette Davis in all of her movies? Sometimes, at night, when my mother went out to smoke and play cards with her Catholic widow friends, I lay on the twin bed in my room, which I had recently decorated in what I called an "oriental style," with white bowls filled with black stones on my desk and nightstand, and a hand-painted Japanese doll on my dresser, a gift from my dull, well-mannered pen pal, Isamu Akamo of Nagasaki. Sometimes, lying there for hours on end, I flipped through the stolen books, trying to memorize the plots of even Bette Davis's least-memorable movies, like *The Girl from 10th Avenue* and *The Big Shakedown,* just as I'd worked only a few years earlier to memorize the *Baltimore Catechism* so I could prepare myself for the sacrament of confirmation, when the archbishop of Washington anointed me with chrism and made me a soldier of Christ.

It was on one of those nights, I imagine, that I got the idea to write to Miss Davis directly, telling myself that I wanted simply to praise her, as was her due, since she was the world's finest living actress, and to tell her how much I loved and admired *The Lonely Life.* And why not? Hadn't my mother's mother spent hours sitting in the basement of her deteriorating Brooklyn brownstone, writing to strangers whom she greatly admired, like Bishop Fulton Sheen, Hedda Hopper, Senator Joe McCarthy, and Grandma

Moses? And besides, wasn't I planning one day to tread the boards myself, a vision emboldened by my having just landed my first dramatic role, as Gentleman #2, in our ninth-grade production of *A Christmas Carol*?

I don't recall how long it took for me to write my letter—maybe weeks, since I remember being careful to choose what I felt were all the right words. Or maybe I wrote it quickly, having already learned as my mother's son how to flatter women, especially if they were vain and aging, as was my mother, born in Brooklyn only a few years after Bette Davis was born in Lowell, Massachusetts, in 1908. After all, it was around the time that I was writing to Bette Davis that I came home from school one afternoon to find my mother standing at the kitchen sink, washing out a lipstick stain from the collar of one of her silk blouses. "Well," she said, turning to look at me in the doorway. "Here I am, removing the last mark of my vanity."

This was my cue to tell her she was beautiful. "Mom," I said, "you have such pretty hair."

"Oh," she said. "Do you think I should cut it?"

In any case, even if I can't recall the actual writing of my letter, I do recall, word-by-word, how the letter began: "Dear Miss Davis," I wrote. "I want to tell you that I consider *The Lonely Life* a masterpiece. The only fault I could possibly find within it is that you take entirely too much blame upon yourself for the failure of your four marriages." I hoped this would please her and perhaps even cause her to reply. I went on to assure her she'd been right to sue her former studio, Warner Bros., for better parts, even if she'd lost, and I commiserated with her over the loss of her mother, Ruthie, who had died the same year as my father. I then briefly described myself as a fourteen-year-old fan and member of the school drama club, working to earn sufficient points for induction into the International Thespian Society. I ended by asking her which of her movies was her personal favorite—*Dark Victory*, perhaps, or *Now, Voyager*?

With the sole exception of my mother, who suggested I mail the letter care of G. P. Putnam's Sons, the autobiography's publisher, I told no one, not even the drama teacher, that I had written Bette Davis a letter. After all, who was there to whom I might make such a confession? The shop teacher? Some vice principal, perhaps? The football coach? And if there had been someone to hear that I'd written to Bette Davis, and how much I adored her, would I have gone on to tell him that my other favorite activities—my sports, if you will—were roller-skating in the basement to the soundtrack of *The Sound of Music* and lip-syncing to Edith Piaf's "Mon Dieu" and "Non, je ne regrette rien"? I kept my secret to myself, wandering alone around my neighborhood, sometimes feeling as if I were on the brink of a whole new life, a life in which I would be escorting Bette Davis to movie premieres and the Academy Awards, a life in which I'd find myself freed at last from the forlorn, treeless subdivision where I'd grown up, each house identical to all the others, with picture windows and zoysia grass yards encircled with chain-link fences. But what, really, were my chances of hearing from Bette Davis? The only other star I'd ever written, requesting a signed photo, was Chuck Connors from *The Rifleman,* and he had never written back.

As it turned out, Miss Davis was more generous, at least compared to Chuck Connors.

One afternoon, maybe a month after mailing my letter, I came home from school to find in the mailbox an 8½ by 10½-inch manila envelope, with my name and address written in large letters across the front with a felt-tip pen, its ink an odd, splashy green, close to the color of an English pea. (As I look again at this same envelope, lying here beside me on my desk as I write, now almost fifty years later, both the envelope and the ink have grown unpleasantly darker.) I recognized the handwriting at once—the blocky cursive; the oversized letters, drawn with what looked to be a hard and definitive hand; the penchant for fat dots suspended above the i's and dramatic underscorings. If I had even a single doubt as to who had inscribed the envelope, the return address rapidly removed it: *From B. Davis, c/o Gottlieb & Schiff, 555 5th Ave, New York City.* I knew from *The Lonely Life* that Gottlieb & Schiff were her lawyers.

Inside, I found an autographed publicity photo—*For Ricky McCann, from Bette Davis*—that has now hung over my desk for more than thirty years, wherever I've lived, and, alongside that, a second envelope containing a letter—four half sheets and a matching envelope, written with the same green ink and engraved at the top with "Honeysuckle Hill," the name of Bette Davis's New England–style house in Bel Air, California, purchased with a loan from Jack Warner against her future earnings for *What Ever Happened to Baby Jane? Dear Master McCann,* it read. *To receive a letter from a young man of your years, with its many perceptive remarks, is quite an experience . . . You talk of how much blame I put upon myself in my book. That was necessary, I felt, in order that I would not appear to be too pleased with myself to the reader.* I knew right away what she meant, of course—the blame had really belonged to others. *That you admire my performances,* she wrote, *makes me very happy and proud. Charlotte* [Davis's character in *Hush . . . Hush, Sweet Charlotte,* an aging, reclusive Southern belle] *was, for the most part, a character I enjoyed very much playing. "All About Eve" is, of course, one of my all time favorites. Most sincerely, Bette Davis.*

Here's what I remember feeling as I lay on my bed, reading the letter over and over again: a sudden, wild glee that Bette Davis, the great Bette Davis, now knew my name and address and who I was in the world, even though I knew myself to be unremarkable and really not too much of anything. I dreamed the letter might redeem me, that I'd show it to Miss Tucci, my drama teacher, who'd soon tell the faculty and my classmates about it, so I'd rapidly become popular as the boy who had Bette Davis as his pen pal. Not that this would really happen—I knew that if I brought the letter to school to show, I'd be taunted for being a sissy and that soon I'd find myself derided by Bucky Trueblood's gang, who'd whisper "faggot" whenever I walked past them in the hall. In fact, I showed it only to my mother, behaving as if I were indifferent to her excitement, perhaps as a way of telling her that I no longer needed her now that she had begun dating again, giving most of her attention to a boorish World War II vet who talked about nothing but the Japs he'd captured while he was stationed in the Pacific. I had Bette Davis now.

I knew what I had to do to gain the leave to write her back, even though she'd asked me no questions about myself to which I might have responded with wit and maybe even candor. I went right back to *The Lonely Life*, searching slowly through its pages and, for the benefit of my future as an actor, underlining passages that I might ask her to explicate more fully, as when she wrote, "Until you're known in my profession as a monster, you're not a star." To these questions, I added an occasional opinion with which I felt sure she'd fervently agree, telling her, for instance, that Miriam Hopkins was out of her depth playing beside her in *Old Acquaintance* and that Joan Crawford was essentially talentless, as well as too broad shouldered and mannish. I imagined these remarks would connect Miss Davis and me and deepen our friendship, having already learned, as my mother's son, that almost any two people could form a tight bond simply by mocking and disparaging a third. I was hopeful that Bette Davis might one day entrust me with a few of her private opinions and make me her confidante, just as my mother had.

In this way, our letter writing went on, back and forth, and in the years that followed—during which time, I am sorry to report, I lost all of Bette Davis's letters to me except for the first and the last—I somehow started to imagine that we'd been pen pals for years. But in truth, there were only maybe four rounds of letters, given and received, making a total of about seven between us, with each of hers written in the same green ink. With each round, the letters got a bit briefer, so the last letter—that's how I thought of it then somehow, as a stopping place, if you will, even if it were just temporary—was two pages long. Here's how it ended: *If you ever find you're in a city where I'm making a movie, please be sure to ring through to the set to arrange a visit.*

Ring through to the set, I remember thinking. *Ring through to the set.* I was sure I had never before heard anything quite so sophisticated as that. *Ring through to the set,* I thought. *Ring through to the set.*

I don't recall the degree to which I missed our correspondence, although I must have missed it somewhat at least. Perhaps I pined for the time when I could still rush home from school, my quick steps sweetened with anticipation, to find a green-inked envelope waiting in the mailbox. Or perhaps I'd begun to tire from the labor it took to keep creating a self—a sincere boy, pliable and sweetly yielding—whom I could present, whether to my mother or Bette Davis, who told me in one of her letters that she could tell that I was a young man "with a lot on the ball" and that I would surely soon find a perfect girlfriend. In any case, I had by that time begun practicing for what I thought of as my "theatrical career," playing Lord Brocklehurst—a prim and humorless aristocrat, endlessly trying and failing to please his brittle, snobbish mother—in our eleventh-grade production of J. M. Barrie's *The Admirable Crichton.* Thanks to J. M. Barrie, I at long last qualified for my induction into the International Thespian Society, Albert Einstein High School chapter. Soon, I was looking into colleges where I might earn a degree in acting, providing such schools met my two requirements: that there be no need to take phys ed, given my dread of football and tumbling, and that the school be neither too near nor too far from home. For my acting audition at the school that was my first choice, in Richmond, Virginia, I prepared an excerpt from my favorite of Lady Macbeth's soliloquies, using gestures I'd learned from Bette Davis to help me as I ranged around the bare stage, my hands moving about so busily that I must have looked as if I were swinging a cigarette as I spoke: *Come, you spirits / that tend on mortal thoughts, unsex me here, / And fill me from the crown to the toe top-full / Of direst cruelty!*

I didn't last long in acting school. In fact, I barely completed the first semester. Although I could not then specify the source of my unhappiness, I blamed it on my teachers, almost all of whom were homosexuals, both young and old. I was nothing like them, I told myself, nothing like them at all, and I was especially nothing like the elderly department chair, Dr. Maurice Holmes, with his pinched face and tight clothes and slender figure, too much like a young girl's. Each time he lifted his right hand to point at something, I felt a sense of horror when I saw his middle finger weighted down, as it was, by a heavy carnelian ring. Perhaps even worse than the homosexuals, however, was the first role I was given, a mere bit part, playing a portly Southern sheriff with only two lines of dialogue. In November, I thought for a moment I was being at last discovered when Dr. Holmes gathered together the whole freshman class to choose two from among us for what he described as "special parts." He pointed first at me—"You!"—and then at Ed Olson, whom everyone knew was not even an actor but rather a major in lighting and sound. *What could Ed Olson and I possibly have in common?* I wondered as we followed Dr. Holmes to his office, as he'd instructed, and it wasn't until after Dr. Holmes shut his office door behind us that it hit me: Ed Olson and I were the two fattest boys in our class. "I am pleased to inform you," Dr. Holmes began, "that I have received a request from the Woolworth Company, which has asked me to hire two seasonal part-timers to share the part of Santa Claus, costumes included."

Could no one see who I really was inside? Had I not been born, as I sometimes believed, to become a great tragedienne? I saw myself as Joan Fontaine dying alone of typhus in Max Ophüls's *Letter from an Unknown Woman*. I saw myself as Susan Hayward, innocent of the murder for which she has been convicted, walking barefoot to her execution in *I Want to Live!* I was Gene Tierney villainously throwing herself down a flight of stairs to cause her own miscarriage in John M. Stahl's *Leave Her to Heaven;* I was Loretta Young, unknowingly married to a Nazi war crimes fugitive in

Orson Welles's *The Stranger.* I was Judith Anderson in *Rebecca,* Gloria Grahame in *The Big Heat,* and Gloria Swanson in *Sunset Boulevard.* I was Shelley Winters and Ida Lupino. I was Dorothy Malone, Patricia Neal, Agnes Moorehead, Vivien Leigh, and even Thelma Ritter. But above all, I always saw myself as Bette Davis, the illustrious and eminent Bette Davis, whether in *Dead Ringer, Of Human Bondage,* or *All About Eve—Fasten your seat belts, it's going to be a bumpy night.*

But perhaps, it occurs to me now, as I write this, the problem was not that I went unseen by others; perhaps the problem was that I was all too disquietingly visible—this heavy, oddly genderless boy who waved his hands about too much as he spoke, his laughter always a bit too eager, too shrill and calculated. One evening, not too long before Christmas vacation, my dorm roommate, Mike O'Boyle—a sophomore who'd already earned a varsity letter from running track—told me we needed to talk. He sat on the edge of his twin bed, clipping his toenails, as he informed me that he'd asked our dorm leader if he could switch rooms and roommates for the next semester. I knew what that meant—it was almost as embarrassing to room with me as it was to be seen with Carlton Folsom, the music major who lived down the hall in a single room he had redecorated himself, with dark velvet drapes and ornate Russian furniture done in the Romanov style. It was rumored of him that he drove more than an hour each weekend to Charlottesville to visit an eccentric, elderly lady who claimed to be the lost Grand Duchess Anastasia of Russia.

I asked Mike if he'd already found someone new to room with.

"No, not yet," he said.

He set his toenail clippers down on his nightstand. Then he lifted his right arm to point at the wall above my bed, to which I had Scotch-taped a large poster of Bette Davis in *All About Eve.* "If you want to help yourself out," he said, "you might start by getting rid of that."

I remember going downstairs and out the door, wandering

the streets for hours, past the monuments the city had erected to Confederate generals and heroes; past blocks of Victorian houses fallen into disrepair; past an all-night drugstore and a local spice factory that always emitted, day or night, the sweet scent of vanilla. By the time I got back to my dorm room, the lights were out and Mike was gone. But I knew what to do: I climbed onto my bed, its mattress barely supported by its broken box spring, and took down the poster. I then carried the poster downstairs to dispose of it in an alleyway Dempster-Dumpster.

Of course, I didn't know then what the years to come would bring. I didn't know that my mother would marry the war vet, or that when I went home to visit, I'd no longer sit with her in the darkened living room, watching old movies on TV. I didn't know that I'd forsake Bette Davis almost altogether, no longer even going to see her new movies—not *The Nanny,* not *The Anniversary,* not *Connecting Rooms.* I didn't know I'd switch my allegiance to movies like *Easy Rider, The Wild Bunch,* and *Dirty Harry,* even if I didn't really like them. I didn't know, when I dropped out of drama school, that I'd find myself hanging with what was then called "the druggy crowd," a mixture of hippies and petty criminals and artists, or that eventually, I'd be hanging with the dealers themselves, a small band of guys, all college dropouts, with whom I began getting together on weekends, getting stoned and watching old horror movies on a portable Philco TV. In time, they asked me to join them on an eighteen-hundred-mile drug run all the way to Albuquerque, where they knew a guy who smuggled bricks of weed up north from Mexico.

And then I was there, in Albuquerque, having breakfast with the guys one morning at a diner, while the one who called himself Wyatt went on and on about how his dick was so big it scared away girls, when I noticed a news item of some personal interest in the *Albuquerque Journal,* which I just happened to be reading. According to the paper, Bette Davis, age sixty-three, had just arrived in

Albuquerque the day before, to make a movie with Ernest Borgnine about a pair of senior citizens who ride around together on a 250cc Triumph TRW Trophy, robbing banks while disguised as hippies.

Bette Davis, I thought. *Bette Davis.* She was right then somewhere not too far from me.

And then I remembered what she had told me in the last of her letters—that if I were ever near any location where she was making a movie, I should ring through to the set and arrange a visit. *Ring through to the set,* I thought. *Ring through to the set.*

For a moment, I wanted to tell my buddies how the great film star Bette Davis had once said this phrase to me. I wanted to ask one of them for a lift to the set, wherever that was, so I could finally meet her—*just for a laugh, of course, just for a laugh at the old lady.*

But I already knew there was no way that I could say these words, not to those gathered at our Formica-topped table. There was no way to say anything at all, at least not without being ridiculed and denigrated. One of the guys would start by saying, "Really? Really? Bette Davis?" And then another would chime in, "Are you kidding me? Bette fucking Davis? Did he really say that?"

The guys were now finishing their breakfasts, pushing the last of their home fries into the small puddles of ketchup left on their plates. Suddenly, the one who called himself Danny said, "Hey, let's score some psilocybin. I know a place in the desert where we can get it."

Then he turned to me and asked, almost as if daring me, "What about you? You coming, too?"

"Of course," I said.

And before long, we were all driving down some sun-baked desert highway in an old, crapped-out Buick Caballero, the windows open and some song by Cream blasting from the AM car radio. It was then that I began to live what was to become for a long time my version of the lonely life.

99/86

Oh my goodness, Barbara Feldon—I so, so loved *Get Smart*. I loved Don Adams as Maxwell Smart. I loved Edward Platt as the Chief (Daddy = failure). I loved the cone of silence as it descended upon Max and the Chief, because even at age seven I knew it was a metaphor for human miscommunication. But really I crushed out completely on Barbara Feldon, Agent 99 (as close as they could get to calling her Agent 69 without calling her that). The purr in her voice; the way she towered over Max, and yet the way he was unaware of her worship (which was the mirror of how we were crushing out on her; she pretended to be oblivious to how much we worshipped her). Her alternate coaxing and chiding of 86. Max as dumb/smart (his stupidity was his gallantry; he got that life is a joke). All the au courant Courrèges and Paco Rabanne outfits she wore, the Vidal Sassoon cut. Ooh la la.

Either *Get Smart* mapped my entire sexual life over the next fifty years, or my psyche got back-formed onto the show. It's very Groucho and Margaret Dumont. All the comedy is on one side— all the Jewishness (Don Adams was raised Catholic, his mother's faith, while his brother was raised Jewish, his father's faith—which is too perfect). Feldon as deadpan WASP, as sex goddess, ice queen as savior, as very subtle (pseudo-oblivious) sadist. The show killed me, still kills me ("missed it by that much").

TONY TULATHIMUTTE

Fantasy Bonds

> *. . . when we are in love with a woman all we are doing is projecting onto her a state of our own self; that, consequently, what is important is not the merit of the woman, but the intensity of that state . . .*
>
> —MARCEL PROUST, *In the Shadow of Young Girls in Flower*

Ask yourself if everything you've loved was real. I don't mean the attachment to a blankie, the fondness for a pet, the Hollywood crush. I mean romantic love for someone who physically does not exist—not forbidden love, but *impossible* love. Cartoons are the most common of these: a straw poll of my acquaintances turns up childhood crushes on Captain Haddock, King Triton from *The Little Mermaid,* the vulpine Robin Hood and Maid Marian; one friend confessed that he not only pined after Gadget from *Chip 'n' Dale Rescue Rangers* but had unearthed a childhood Disney coloring book where he'd expressed his devotion by drawing brown and yellow torrents fluming from Gadget's groin.

Still, cartoons have a lot of substance and definition to them; Gadget is a likable enough anthropomorph with a voice and a well-defined personality and big blue eyes; you can see how a kid might get ideas. I sure did, in 1991, with an unbalanced imagination even by seven-year-old standards. I'd recently been through some rough breakups with Daisy Duck and Jessica Rabbit, and I was looking for something real.

A few afternoons a week I'd walk up the street to play video games with Arian, an older Iraqi-American kid. We, two of the very few Asians in the racial tundra of our western Massachusetts suburb, would sit in his room in front of his fourteen-inch TV, tethered to a Super Nintendo. The Gulf War (nicknamed "the Video Game War" for its live broadcasts of combat) had ended a few months earlier, and I'd imagined that this was why his mother looked so mournful—bombings, invasion, not two chubby boys giving their brains a digital *sous-vide,* grimacing when she brought in juice and cheese crackers on a tray.

One afternoon he invited me over to watch him play *Final Fantasy II,*[*] an early entry in the long-running role-playing franchise. He was already halfway through the game, so I had no sense of the story, characters, or mechanics—not that I needed any to keep me staring at the four squat, unblinking characters lined up, sprites[†] of perhaps forty pixels each, fighting an enormous purple knight. The knight almost succeeded in killing them all, until a female mage entered, whose green leotard matched her green angel-sleeved cape, boots, and Farrah Fawcett hair swoop.

"Who's that?" I asked Arian, tapping on the screen, because I knew he hated that.

"Rydia," he said.

"Who's that?"

"A girl."

"What's she like?"

He wore the dawning look of the gamer whose consciousness is returning through the glass. "Dude, shut up."

We passed the next few hours inputting plinky, chirpy menu commands to slay monsters with names like FatalEye and EvilWall, who sizzled when they died. I got up from my chair to get a closer look, holding my eye on the green sprite twitching her fingers and

---

[*] Known these days as *Final Fantasy IV* for inane localization reasons.

[†] FYI for nongamers: A "sprite" is the animated 2-D image that denotes a character, not a fairy or a soda.

incanting. Stashed somewhere in Arian's room was an issue of *Playboy* we'd once browsed with dwindling interest, as they were still, noninteractive photos. Arian invented a game where we'd take turns holding up the centerfold while the other shot at it with an NES Zapper pistol, but this bored us quickly, thank god.

I left Arian's house feeling silent and inward, undeterred by the logistics of imagining romance with a sixteen-bit sprite, of holding a four-pixel hand—filling in blanks is no challenge for a second grader. Nor did I dwell on the fact that she couldn't know I existed; this was also nothing new. (Did I mention Arian was my only friend?) Mostly I was excited that I'd discovered an absolutely new form of love.

A few months later I scored *Final Fantasy II* as a birthday gift and plowed through it in the Styrofoam-ceilinged basement, the Underworld where I spent my childhood. I was surprised to find that Rydia is, when you first meet her, seven years old (age-appropriate!); that the main protagonist orphans her by accidentally destroying her hometown of Mist and becomes her caretaker; that she gets lost at sea and washes up in the Underworld, where time passes faster, so that at your next encounter she's grown into an adult.

What, indeed, was she like? Developed in the teenage years of video games, *FFII*'s characterization is crude and flat but still entrancingly suggestive to a kid. Like all the other characters, Rydia bows her head when sad, twirls when happy, fist-pumps in victory, and scolds people with a bonk to the head. Spell-casting surrounds her in a circular strobe. She descends from a tribe of magical "Callers" who summon creatures from the Underworld, to whom they are specially bonded. To someone with his own special bond for an otherworldly creature, it was not difficult to see that Rydia was an allegory for the player.

There's not much else to say about her. This was as close as it got to being infatuated with absolutely nothing, with an idea—thus, a handy distillation of crushhood. Broadly speaking, a crush works like this: you meet or see someone you know scarcely anything about, and you connect the dots with your own idealized hopes, not necessarily aware you're doing it. You experience a kind of private Beatlemania that launches you into a thrall of fact-finding and photo-gazing, and potentially get to know your crush. Over time, the exposure either disillusions you or complicates/mellows/deepens to something like actual love, once the aura of crushhood is dispelled enough to see the real person.

Celebrities obviously cater to this impulse: they're unattainable strangers whose best images and qualities we're routinely exposed to, charging them with watchedness, whether or not there's anything there. They can induce panic attacks by their mere presence, even without admiration. (A former student of mine said she cried when she met Redfoo from LMFAO at the airport. I asked her if she was a fan of his: "Ew.") "We worship perfection because we can't have it," wrote Fernando Pessoa, "if we had it, we would reject it."

A crush on a video game character is something different; the interactivity complicates the distance, the unattainability. To nurture feelings for a video game character is at once a form of Pygmalionic self-worship, domineering possession, and spiritual infusion. If infatuation compels you to invent an inner life for someone, with a video game crush, you literally become that inner life. It's not exactly true that you "are" your character; really you *control* a character, functioning as a surrogate soul, and consequently most games share a subtle element of domination. You can bid your characters to jump on command, walk off a cliff, or murder innocent people, and they generally have no say in the matter; as graphics improved and games became more open-ended, the BDSM ramifications became troublingly clear. I know I'm not the only teenager who spent minutes intricately backing Lara Croft up against a wall so that the camera would swing around and reveal the sharp ridge of her chest, which otherwise faced away. (Sometimes the camera would get crowded out and reposition itself inside Lara's body, reminding the player that 3-D characters are literally hollow, pure surface.)

I wasn't quite so aggressive with Rydia, partly because the things you could do with her were limited. You could fight and cast spells; you make her the party leader, so that her sprite displayed while you walked around. But mostly I doted, equipping her with the rarest wands and robes, and keeping her alive at all costs (though characters in *FFII* don't die—they "swoon"). Conversely I let her would-be suitor, a pathetic ninja lothario named Edge, stay good and swooned. When I visited Arian I was gratified to see that his Rydia was pathetically underfed: he didn't care as much.

This was enough to sustain the infatuation for a few months, though it struck me even then as a puerile fantasy to be outgrown, and strikes me even now as pretty regressive, being drawn to an empty icon of femininity, a virtual blow-up doll. I once worried that my childish attachments had transferred into adulthood—what the psychologist Robert Firestone called the "fantasy bond"—and had glitched some deep kernel of affection in me. Was this why, in the following decades, I would be drawn to women *because* they didn't like me, why flirty correspondences lost their shimmer face-to-face, or why I'd be accused of overglorifying relationships? Later, when I realized that nearly everyone did all of those things, I decided the truth was probably even sadder: that love doesn't inhere in the beloved, it is only elicited, and so to fall for a fingerless sixteen-bit sprite with no last name was as unreal as any infatuation.

My thing for Rydia didn't end with the discovery of any disillusioning flaw or nuance (she had none), but with the opposite: she became perfect. At level 99, clad in Ribbon and Stardust Rod, all spells acquired, she was immortal and self-sufficient. I had paced for hours in a tiny room in the core of the Moon to fight the rare PinkPuffs whose tails you could trade to a tiny blacksmith for legendary Adamant armor. There was nothing more I could do for her. Of course I could just replay the game from the beginning, and did several times, but this only felt like the nostalgic revisitation of a past relationship. She would never change.

The game's finale, after one defeats Zeromus the evil Lunarian, is a montage of each character's fate. We visit Rydia in an Underworld catacomb, receiving praise from the king and queen. A baby monster, robed and faceless like a Jawa, interrupts to ask her why Rydia doesn't have fangs: "Are we different?"

"Come on! There's nothing different between us," she replies. When the king praises her beauty, she demurs: "The heart is what's important."

Of course I still own the game and could go looking for her at any moment of her life—her tragic childhood, the adolescence that shot by unseen, or her adulthood among monsters in the Underworld, where time passes faster—but then I would only find myself.

KARIN TANABE

Mom, I Want to Marry a Murderer

A floppy-haired youth between the ages of eleven and eighteen with gyrating boy-band hips: that's who I was supposed to have a crush on when I was ten years old. But it didn't work out that way. From the second I watched *The Godfather: Part III,* my heart belonged to Andy Garcia.

His name alone conjures up both preppy lacrosse players with a penchant for Yuengling and sultry nights in Havana. Of course his real name is Andrés Arturo García Menéndez, but I didn't know that when I was ten. Andy Garcia was fine with me, and Andy Garcia playing the gun-loving mobster Vincent Corleone was even better.

The first time I saw him on-screen, he was thirty-four years old; his hair was slicked back, showing off his Dracula-esque hairline; and his dark eyes seemed to womanize from Little Italy to Sicily even when closed. Vincent—no, Vincenzo, Vincenzo Corleone. The outsider, the bastard son, the one who carries on a relationship with his first cousin consummated after making gnocchi. The kissing cousins thing didn't weird me out when I was ten for I fully understood how Sofia Coppola could fall for that man, blood relative and all.

So I watched the movie obsessively and took home some important life lessons in the process. I learned that if a man is good-looking enough, he can pull off wearing an open, Joan Collins–approved, red silk robe and that it looks especially good if paired with a large handgun. I learned that Andy Garcia has enough chest hair to knit a turtleneck with, and that he has very sharp bicuspids, so sharp they can puncture human flesh in a jiffy. He also, when playing the future don, prefers to make love on red bedsheets, can kill people as easily as he can swat a fly, and might want to look into anger management classes.

My babysitter in the early nineties had a real problem with my love of *The Godfather: Part III* and lived in fear that I would end up a homicidal maniac because of it. Even tweenage, I was starting to get antsy with the picturesque suburban neighborhood I lived in outside of Washington, DC, full of happy, safe tax attorneys and their mini-me children who wanted to go on and do happy, safe things. There had to be other kinds of men out there, edgy, dangerous older men who were never members of their neighborhood swim teams and didn't aspire to law-abiding careers. This love of what she called "deranged animal men" caused my babysitter Sarah to frantically look through my belongings for knives or evidence of prison correspondence.

"What do you even know about Andy Garcia?" she asked me as I rubbed my hands together with glee as we watched Andy shoot two would-be assassins while nearly naked.

"I know the most important thing," I said, running to my room. I came back holding a piece of pink notebook paper. "I know his agent's address. See?" I said, pointing to the "c/o Hollywood Studios" address. "I don't need to know anything else. I'll just write to him and ask him the questions."

"He won't write back. They never do," she said with the wisdom of a sixteen-year-old.

The next time Sarah came over she had an entire file on Andy Garcia in her backpack, which she had prepared for me in her high school library.

"Did you know he was born with an undeveloped conjoined twin attached to his shoulder?" she asked, taking out her paperwork.

"What are you talking about?" I asked nervously.

"Here, I drew you a picture," she said, handing me a piece of oversized printer paper.

I looked down at the drawing, which was surprisingly detailed. "That looks like a panda sitting on his shoulder," I said, staring at the piece of bamboo it was holding.

"Well, it looked like an undeveloped human at first," she said, examining her artwork. "It had human features that weren't quite all there. Then I got the idea to call it Pandy Garcia and I turned it into a panda. I'm going to make a comic strip about him."

"Thanks," I said, taking it away from her.

"Yes, you should thank me. I'm saving you from having a crush on an old man who was born with an alien attached to his body."

"It's not an alien!" I said, looking down at Pandy Garcia. I loved that Andy had a flaw. His flawesome flaw. "Andy can handle anything, even a dead twin. He went from family reject to Don Corleone in a few short months!"

"You have to remember, Andy Garcia is not Vincent Corleone, he's just playing the character. There's a difference. The real Andy Garcia could be very dull."

I was sure he wasn't.

"I love both Andy Garcia the man and Andy Garcia playing Vincent Corleone," I explained.

"But you can't love him!" she said, pointing at the television. "He's a murderer. See, he just killed someone while riding a horse."

"That was Joey Zasa, the enemy," I explained, watching Andy smile like a maniac after he pumped his nemesis full of lead. "And of course I can love him. He's a sex machine."

"A what?" she said anxiously. "Where did you learn the term 'sex machine'?"

"*Soul Train,*" I said, shoving blue Pixy Stix dust into my mouth.

She rolled her eyes and ejected *The Godfather: Part III* from the VCR. "Listen . . . ," she said, pulling a VHS copy of Disney's *The*

Little Mermaid out of her bag. "Watch this instead or your parents are going to fire me and I like my eight dollars an hour." She popped the cassette in and pulled my sugar rush away.

Together we ate food that fell from an actual tree and watched as a mermaid named Ariel became a human after being tormented by a chubby octopus woman and randomly befriending a Jamaican crab. There was also some nearly blue-haired guy involved who had enormous calves.

"He's a cartoon," I said, pointing out the obvious. "You really want me to be in love with a drawing instead of a real person? I might as well fall in love with Pandy Garcia."

"Yes," said Sarah, humming along to the musical numbers. "I really do."

Prince Eric seemed like a puffy pirate-shirt-wearing loser compared to Vincent Corleone, but still, babysitters are wise, and I listened to Sarah and tried my best to lust after a drawing of a man in capri pants.

Something about Sarah's words that day must have made an impression on me, because though my Andy Garcia crush never faded, I did manage to date pretty nice guys during my teenage years. One of the first penises I ever saw was even attached to a preacher's son.

Then my junior year abroad in college happened.

Like any wise young woman who likes luxury and is afraid of bugs, I did my year in hard-knocks Paris, France, where I often found myself dancing in *les discothèques* with *les gentlemens*. One night I met a dashing man at a club on the Champs-Élysées. His name was Bruno, and he worked in a casino, had great cheekbones, and was really generous with the vodka.

Things between Bruno and me heated up that spring, and when summer came rolling in, he was heading back to his father's house in Porto-Vecchio, Corsica, and invited me and my friend Mary-Alice to join him.

Bruno called Corsica heaven on earth. "We don't like main-land influences," he explained. "Too ugly. If someone tries to open a McDonald's, we blow it up."

It sounded extreme but what did I know about urban planning?

On our first night, unable to sleep, I crawled out of Bruno's bed and knocked on Mary-Alice's door to see if she was still awake. She hissed at me to join her at the window.

"You have to see this," she said. Together, we watched as five black Mercedes sedans drove up the property's long driveway. The doors opened and a dozen men entered the house.

"So, Bruno's dad is popular," I said, moving away from the window.

"More like Bruno's dad is in the Corsican Mafia," she said, her nose to the glass.

"No way," I countered. "They're not Italian. This is Corsica."

"There's a huge Mafia in Corsica!" Mary-Alice said, correcting me. "Huge."

I went back to Bruno's room, where he was sleeping peacefully, a picture of his late mother next to his bed. Mary-Alice had to be wrong.

Before we went out the following day, Bruno led me upstairs alone.

"I just want to get some money for tonight," he explained. We walked over to the far wall of the living room, where a painting of a maniacal-looking goat playing the flute was featured. He pushed the frame and it slid to the side, revealing a safe embedded into the wall. Inside were piles of five-hundred-franc notes, tied together in thick bundles. He took out the equivalent of three thousand dollars, closed up the operation, and led me outside.

I was dating a Mafia scion.

How, after so many years of trying to avoid bad-boy types, had I stumbled into the arms of the mob? It had to be Andy Garcia's fault.

Call it naïveté or just the fulfillment of my childhood dream, but I had a very good time in Corsica and managed to get off the island without doing anything illegal. By fall, I was back in college in New York State and suddenly September 11, 2001, was upon us.

A few hours after the planes crashed into the World Trade Center, my cell phone rang. I lifted up the antenna and looked at the "Unavailable" caller ID before saying hello. A deep French voice came over the airwaves. *"T'es vivante?"*—*Are you alive?*—he asked. *"Oui,"* I replied, before the line went dead. It was Bruno, my mafioso.

I remember so much about being on a college campus on September 11. As the school was just up the Hudson from Manhattan, many students had family in the city and were rightfully distraught. I remember my professor walking into my art history class in tears, telling us to leave and call our loved ones. I remember my Islamic studies teacher saying that she thought it was an important day to hold class. But I also remember that phone call, the only one that reached me that day, and the reassurance it brought. The telephone lines all over New York were tied up, but somehow, a call from Corsica made it through. As Andy Garcia taught me, the Mafia really can get the job done.

PART 8

Over It!

Does your first celebrity crush ever really go away, or do you hold a lifelong torch? For some of our contributors, the answer is definitely: they go away. In fact, they're a little bit mortified when they take a cold, hard look back at the celebrity crush that once made them weak in the knees.

CATHY ALTER

Puppy Love

I t was 1972 and Donny Osmond's "Puppy Love" was blowing up the charts. I was a first grader, about to turn seven, and could not get enough of it. Luckily, the song was on heavy rotation on the radio station my mother favored and that she listened to in our kitchen as she made my brother and me breakfast or in her car as she drove us around to get gas or pick up a head of lettuce.

When Donny's sweet voice hit the airwaves, all conversation in the car or around the table ceased while I sang along, "And they call it puppy love."

I was not one of those performing, center-of-attention kind of kids. Quiet and serious, I preferred sitting alone during recess and drawing pictures of horses.

So this sudden need to burst into song was greeted by my mother with great fanfare. She was known to tap-dance through the first floor of our house and spent Sunday afternoons watching forties movie musicals so she must have figured her influence was finally starting to take effect.

It wasn't long before I transferred a love of the song to a love for the singer. Donny was cute, in a way that was doll-like and familiar. Big eyes, even bigger teeth, and a hairdo unlike that of most of the boys I knew, including my brother. My mother called my brother's haircut the bowl cut, like someone had placed a small mixing bowl over my brother's blond head and just cut around the edges. Donny's hair was thick, like my brother's, but dark brown and coiffed more carefully, his waves framing his face like the hair on the male mannequins at Lord & Taylor.

"What happened to Bobby Sherman?" my mother eventually asked.

My traitor's heart was on the move. Before Donny, I had fallen hard for the hair-feathering and neckerchief-wearing Sherman after seeing him guest-star on *The Partridge Family*. I'm still not sure what a six-year-old girl sees in a man with an Adam's apple other than on an aesthetic level. Perhaps Bobby was unthreatening in his soft features and dimples. Perhaps one of my babysitters had come over with a *Teen Beat* magazine and told me she liked him best. More than likely, one of my friends had a Bobby Sherman lunch box and I had gazed upon his face on a daily basis, and in the same way a duck patterns on its mother, I had latched on to Bobby Sherman.

My mother understood devotion. When I found a bunch of old Elvis Presley 45s in my grandparents' basement, she told me that in junior high school she had been the Connecticut chapter president of the Elvis Presley fan club. And even after her father punished her when she told him she thought Sidney Poitier was handsome (a negro!), she refused to forsake her man, hanging pictures of him in her bedroom and humming "To Sir with Love" whenever my grandfather was within earshot.

My mother also understood the fickleness of children and especially the changing winds of her own daughter. I was famous for only wanting one thing—to wear a particular red wool dress for days on end or to eat oatmeal at every meal for a month straight—only to change course and reject the things I had come to love entirely.

For now, I loved Donny Osmond and my mother supported this yearning unconditionally.

In fact, my mother encouraged my crush on Donny by encouraging what would eventually take root and turn into a lasting love: writing.

"You should send him a letter," she told me. "I bet he'll write you back."

That was all I needed to hear. We went to King's, the local five-and-dime store, to select a box of stationery, purple of course, which Donny had revealed to be his favorite color in a much pored-over *Teen Beat* interview. Finally, my mother and I sat down to compose this letter. I wrote all that was in my six-year-old heart:

> *Dear Donny,*
> *I love you.*
> *Love,*
> *Cathy*

My letter-writing campaign continued daily and for months and through multiple boxes of stationery—but the letters were always the same.

> *Dear Donny,*
> *I love you.*
> *Love,*
> *Cathy*

Every night after dinner my mother and I would sit down to write. It always started with the same question.

"How do you spell 'Dear'?" I'd ask my mother, who would sometimes use my letter-writing time to polish her nails with a few coats of Revlon's Love That Red, her trademark color. After she spelled it out, I'd glide over the word "Donny" until the next road-block. "And how do you spell 'love'?" Once she spelled that word for me, I could refer back to it in my sign-off, since the word appeared twice in my letter, the best word to convey everything I had to say. After a few weeks, I no longer needed to ask my mother how to spell words, but she still sat next to me every evening, either polishing her long, oval nails or just watching me at work. The radio was constantly on and if we heard "Puppy Love," we looked up from our respective tasks and smiled at each other.

"That's a good sign!" my mother always said. And I believed her.

After I had carefully folded the letter into the envelope and licked it shut, my mother would take over and add the address. I didn't trust my little-girl handwriting to make it all the way to Utah, home of the Osmond fan club. We found the address listed in the back of *Teen Beat* magazine, along with the addresses of other heartthrobs, should I have chosen to write to them, as well.

Every morning, my mother would make a big show of putting a stamp on the envelope and leaving it in our front mailbox for Tommy the postman to retrieve. This just made the whole experience even more special since I adored Tommy, who had a tattoo of a mermaid splashed across his arm. If he was in the mood and had the time, Tommy would roll up his sleeve and say, "Wanna see her swim?" Then he'd flex his bicep a few times, causing the mermaid's tail to swish back and forth.

Thinking Donny's response would be instantaneous, I religiously began checking the mail when I got home from school, my heart sinking each day that passed without a glimpse of correspondence from Osmond headquarters.

"Utah is far away," my mother said, trying to console me.

The months of waiting only made my stirrings more desperate. As December approached, my first-grade teacher, Miss King, went into full-on Christmas mode and crocheted tiny candy canes onto which she threaded safety pins so that we could wear them on our sweaters. I loved my teacher in the way that most little girls love their first teachers, so my candy cane was surgically attached to my body all month long. Miss King also got us thinking about presents. One day, she passed out sheets of neatly ruled paper. "I want you to write down the thing you want most for Christmas."

This brought out a lot of discussion among my classmates. The girls debated the merits of brunette Crissy versus blond Velvet, *the* dolls of the day, whose locks would grow when you pushed in their belly buttons and yanked on their ponytails. Their hair would retreat when you cranked the small wheel protruding from their backs. Boys shouted out a wish list of G.I. Joes and Tonka trucks.

I would have none of it. After neatly printing my name and then writing it in cursive, I got right to the task at hand.

"I want," I wrote as neatly as I could, "Donny Osmond."

The paper, now yellowed, still resides in the frame in which my mother placed it. Miss King's pencil-drawn star is still shining brightly from the top right corner of the page. I have it displayed on my desk, above my computer, a reminder that writing is most powerful when it gets right to the point. It's also a reminder of my mother's delight in me, a delight that was often challenged as I matured into a sullen teen.

But there was another December birthday even more important than Jesus's. Donny Osmond would be celebrating his own birthday on December 9. He had yet to write me back, despite my letter-a-day habit, and I knew it was finally time to up the ante and do something bold. Donny-getting bold.

Naturally, I knew from devouring *Teen Beat* magazine that whatever Donny might like would have to be purple. Photographs always showed him wearing his trademark purple socks. I decided to go shopping and get him something to match. And when I say "go shopping," I mean, "peruse the selection in my father's closet and steal something."

I made a beeline for his rotating tie tree and spun it around until I found what I was looking for: a lime-green and lilac striped tie. Because this was the seventies, its width was of clown proportions. It wasn't solid purple, but, I should mention, it was velvet, which ran a close second in my book.

I don't remember if I kept the tie hidden from my father until after dinner, when he retired to the den to smoke his customary cigar and watch the evening news. I don't remember if, as soon as he left the room, I ran upstairs and pulled the tie out from under my pillow and brought it back downstairs. I may have done that. Or I may have kept my crime out in the open, casually presenting the tie to my mother and asking for help rolling it into the envelope. Whatever the scenario, my mother was my coconspirator. That tie went to Utah.

My father never missed it and I'm guessing my mother was happy to see it go. I tended to go for flashy and sparkly things when I was young and this tie did not disappoint.

It also did the trick, because not long after I sent the tie, I came home from school to find a slim white envelope waiting for me. My mother had set it on the kitchen table, in front of my usual seat, the same seat from which I wrote all of those love letters. I remember seeing "Osmond" in the preprinted return address and looking back and forth from the letter in my hand to the look of pure happiness on my mother's face. It was the first time—but certainly not the last—I would cry tears of joy. My reward was literally in hand, but now, nearly forty years later, it is my mother's face that I remember more. Beautiful and smiling, and all because of what we had done together.

I wish I could freeze that moment—the sweet and perfect moment of possibility before it all went to pot. Because I had to spoil that moment and open the envelope. And to this day, I still feel the anger rising when I remember what was contained inside.

A form letter. At the time my mother explained it using the word "mimeographed." It was a boilerplate sort of thing, written—and I use that verb loosely—in Donny's auto-scribed hand. The letter made no mention of my dedicated correspondence. Instead, it offered, in cheerful language, the amazing opportunity to join

Donny's official, Donny-approved fan club. I don't remember one word of it. I do remember checking to see if the signature was real. I licked my finger and ran it along Donny's name. It didn't smudge. I was outraged.

I also remember that I turned to my mother and said, "This is all I get?" In all honesty, I think I was expecting to open the envelope to find an engagement ring taped to the letter. And then I cried, looking toward my mother for answers.

She again came to the rescue, gently explaining how famous people like Donny get busy, since there must be lots of people writing him letters and so, she told me, he needed to hire people to help answer all the letters he received. But, she assured me, he must have received all of my letters, including the tie, in order to write me back.

I didn't care. I felt like a total dupe, even in my newly minted eighth year of life. How dare Donny not send me one of those purple teddy bears I had seen him clutching in a recent *Teen Beat* spread? How dare he not even bother to write his own name after what felt like the hundreds of times I had written my own at the bottom of my letters?

There were more boys after Donny, of course. More disappointments and, eventually, some successes. When I moved to New York City after college and experienced my first real betrayal, it was my mother who wrote to me. "Beware of snakes in the grass," she warned, a hand-drawn serpent, forked tongue and all, accompanying her proclamation. "You are a smart and funny and beautiful woman who deserves a lot better." Like my Christmas request for Donny Osmond, I have also saved this letter, and now that my mother can no longer speak, suffering from a rare form of dementia that robs those afflicted of language, I pull it out on occasion just to hear her voice.

I take comfort in knowing that my mother was fully present when I finally, at age thirty-nine, got love right. Handsome and forthright, with a goofy vision to build what he calls a "robot farm," Karl is the embodiment of what all those love songs are really about. And when I think of the lasting power of love—so intensely pure and undiluted—I think of my mother and my mind instantly returns to that image of her in our kitchen, sitting next to me and spelling out the very word.

JULIA PIERPONT

Still Rivers Run Deep

My first kiss wasn't with Rivers Cuomo, but it was in front of him, at a Weezer concert during the band's "Midget" tour. I can't for the life of me remember why the tour was called that, nor can I remember the lucky guy's name—Mark? Matthew? Yehuda?—only that he looked vaguely like Zack Morris minus the lemon-juice highlights and that he knew all the lines to "My Name Is Jonas," which was very much enough for me. When the show was over he wandered off with a group of boys all grinning and nudging one another, and my friend Sarah's mom took us home in an SUV, complaining that our clothes smelled like pot smoke.

Adolescence is dominated by two very distinct types of crushes. There are the public ones, crushes that take place in the backs of school buses over tattered issues of *Tiger Beat*. Within my age group these were your Devon Sawas, your Rider Strongs, your Leos. We pawed at pictures of JTT shirtless under a pair of overalls, a peace sign (*he loves peace!*) on a cord around his neck (never mind that his prepubescent torso was indistinguishable from any of ours).

Then there are private crushes. I found Rivers a few years later, during the era of dial-up and AOL, when "Google" was still an awkward word to say. I was thirteen and someone on a message board mentioned the song "Across the Sea," off Weezer's long-underrated but now highly acclaimed sophomore album, *Pinkerton*. I downloaded the song, probably off Napster, which probably took no fewer than seventeen minutes. According to the Internet's Weezerpedia,

"Across the Sea" is "one of the most emotionally charged songs in the entire Weezer canon." Is it *ever.*

"Across the Sea" turns out to have been the perfect gateway drug for my affection, as the song is itself about serious celebrity crushing. Written in response to a fan letter Rivers received, it begins, "You are eighteen-year-old girl who live in small city of Japan" (though it's easy to imagine that "eighteen" was really more like "fourteen"). (It's perhaps worth noting that Japanese girls, or half-Japanese girls, as evidenced in the song "El Scorcho," are kind of a thing for Rivers; I would soon come to bemoan my ethnic disadvantage.) Rivers wonders what clothes the girl wears to school, how she decorates her room, and how she *touches herself,* which was exhilarating in an embarrassing way to my baby ears. The song's climax—"As if I could live on words and dreams and a million screams / Oh, how I need a hand in mine to feel"—gave me full-body shivers under my headphones in the school stairwell between classes.

I got their entire discography at the Tower Records near Lincoln Center—which at the time amounted to only two records: *Pinkerton* and their debut album, self-titled but differentiated as *Blue.* I still didn't know what the voice behind these songs looked like, and I remember studying the faces of the four-man lineup on the cover of *Blue* and thinking, If that's *the guy who wrote these songs, I'm in trouble. I'm in* love.

What did I love about Rivers? Clean-shaven in Buddy Holly glasses and knit sweaters, he could have filled any of the empty chairs in the back row of Algebra II. Rivers was cute and he was safe. If I was shy, he was shyer. If I was misunderstood—that adolescent cliché—he was more so. I began saving Rivers JPEGs to a folder on my computer—the Internet still seemed like a place where things could disappear, and I wanted my own records for safekeeping, a digitized version of the teeny-bopper magazines I'd outgrown. I amassed hundreds of files: fan-uploaded photographs of the band, the =W= emblazoned on drummer Pat Wilson's kit, a crumpled set list. Faded scans of a bowl-cutted young Rivers alongside his brother, Leaves, on the ashram farm where they grew up. Fan-made logos with their catchphrase, "If it's too loud, turn it down," drawn in MS Paint. Whatever I could get my mouse on.

Also, I bought everything. First comes crush, then comes commerce. I bought guitar tabs I couldn't read and a blue guitar I couldn't play (not least of all because I'm left-handed). I bought Weezer car decals, though my family had no car, and a Weezer lunch box, where I kept hair ties. When the band's third album came out I bought that, too, on CD as well as on vinyl, a conspicuous lime-green addition to my parents' record collection.

Anyone who knows Weezer's music will tell you that this third album, another self-titled release that's called *Green,* signaled a departure for the band. While *Blue* is raucous and varied, *Pinkerton* is uniformly dark, even when buoyed by upbeat melodies. The lyrics betray a deeply personal, deeply autobiographical time in Rivers's life, written mostly while he was on rock star sabbatical at Harvard, out of the limelight and enduring a medieval-sounding surgical procedure that had to do with one of his legs having grown shorter than the other and that may have involved a crank. *Pinkerton* was a commercial flop; *Rolling Stone* readers voted it the third-worst album of 1996. Though it was well on its way to being redeemed—in 2002, those same readers voted it the sixteenth-greatest album *of all time*—Rivers seemed to have taken the criticism to heart, disowning the record as "a hugely painful mistake that happened in front of hundreds of thousands of people."

Green signaled not merely a return to the more playful stylings of *Blue* but something more aggressive: pep in the extreme. The songs were short and punchy and fun, but they didn't make me feel a thing. Not long after that, Rivers began describing in interviews his latest songwriting efforts, which involved spreadsheets and analyses of other artists, aimed at getting hit-making down to a science. This evolution was so obviously a response to the poor reception of the band's last, and rawest, album; Rivers no longer trusted the world with his feelings. This was not the musician I'd fallen in love with, but it only made me love him more: I was fourteen, he was thirty, and I wanted to save him.

I saw Weezer in concert again a couple of years ago, at an outdoor music festival in Atlanta, between episodes of pouring rain. In my plastic poncho I bobbed along, well above the median age in the weed-smoked air. And you know what? The band looked a little old, too. Drummer Pat wore a Bluth's Original Frozen Banana Stand shirt, a respectable if tired nod to *Arrested Development*. Rivers finally allowed a different *Pinkerton* song on the set list, "El Scorcho," which I never thought I'd hear performed live. The crowd was too young for it; they liked songs from the new albums, tracks I've never heard whose titles I was vaguely suspicious of, like "Pork and Beans."

The big relief (that's also sad) about childhood crushes is that they end. The world doesn't look like it did. The girl whose mother drove us home from the concert moved to Cairo. There is no Napster anymore, there is no need to download anything now: we stream; we have clouds. Of course, there's no Tower Records in New York either, and that's too bad, even if the public headphones were rumored to carry head lice.

But about a month ago I played a game called "Drinkerton" with some friends from graduate school. It's a drinking game that could work with most any album, but standing in a room surrounded by people singing "Across the Sea," that was real camaraderie. I felt like I'd found the people I wanted to know at fourteen. Like I was in the right place.

And there's the fact that you can still get *Tiger Beat* delivered, to your door, in print. Adolescent girls and their affinity for collage will save print media yet.

CAROLINE KEPNES

Brian Austin Green: Pen Pal

I am a big proponent of the definition of fiction, as in: *It's a made-up story. It's not a diary.* I was all about this the summer before my first novel *You* debuted. When I started writing this series of voicey thrillers from the perspective of a charming sociopath named Joe Goldberg, I didn't realize the extent to which people would be curious about the whole girl-writes-boy thing. Particularly when said male character is a charming sociopath. Yes, in addition to reading lots of Paula Fox books and watching *Hannah and Her Sisters,* Joe stalks and murders people, but not arbitrarily. He does this for love! Anyway, when you create this kind of character, people wonder where it comes from. It's human nature. I get it. Still, it was eating at me, my aunt Carole calling me "Freak Caroline" instead of "Sweet Caroline," the implication that I must be off to write someone so off. Grr.

Also, I was back home on Cape Cod in the house where I grew up, in the bedroom where I spent the first eighteen years of my life. So you think about this shit even more when you're at the source. I couldn't sleep and I was rummaging through my old bedroom, the way you do when you realize that you use your imagination to lock people up in basements and torture them. I needed to flip through my diaries from school. I needed the relief, the confirmation that I had been just another boy-crazy girl, no secret murders.

Diaries are comforting. I wrote mostly about boys, lists of boys. I did boy-math. I calculated my romantic potential based on the numerical values of the letters in our names. The algorithms and yearning, page after page of obsessive analytics about why I liked this one more than that one, which one I would choose in the event of a natural disaster, what shirt this one wore that brought out the color of his hair.

I used to look at these diaries and feel guilty. Why did I *only* write about boys? Why was I so damn obsessive? Why couldn't I be like those filmmakers, mostly men, the ones who talk about shooting movies on Super 8 and obsess over Steven Spielberg? (Hi, Eli Roth.) Well, I think you grow up and get used to yourself, but I won't lie. I think I'll always hope to discover a few pages were stuck together, pages where I expounded on Laura Ingalls Wilder's prose instead of so-and-so's blue-and-white shirt and the fact that he might have been looking at me while we were singing "The Greatest Love of All" in chorus. But of course I never will. A diary doesn't evolve. It's a Dead Sea Scroll. It's you, naked.

And I was right. My diaries were proof that my novel was just a made-up story. I never stalked anyone. I was a nice little girl. I just wanted love. I didn't do anything bad or crazy and I could go to sleep. But then I spotted something under the bed, a tinted-blue plastic storage box. My stomach churned. I had a bad feeling about that box, like it was going to take all my inner peace away. But I had to look. Archaeologists have to dig. You can't ignore things just because they might upset you. And when I pulled this box out and opened it, oh yes, it did upset me. It derailed me. It was my Brian Austin Green box. I had forgotten all about this damn box. Inside there were signed pictures, no big whoop. But below those pictures there were *letters* from Brian. I cringed. I was lying. The word isn't *forgot*. No. I blocked this shit out, the summer I went a little fucking crazy and tried to seduce Brian Austin Green through snail mail. Ick. Bad. Ick.

Letters from anyone are scarier than your diaries. What you write under lock and key is yours and yours alone (and your mom's, probably). But letters reveal what you said to someone else. Letters contain your truth, your lies, your strategy. I hadn't even opened the envelopes yet but already I was having flashbacks induced by his bright blue name stamp on the cover of every envelope: BRIAN. Oh, the way I wanted him to fly to Cape Cod and dance with me in front of the other boys at school so that they would all realize I was beautiful and awesome. I felt that a famous boyfriend would make everything better. And worse, I felt like this was completely doable. You remember your mind, like it or not.

In case you didn't know, Brian Austin Green was a child actor. He was the cutest guy on planet Earth, son of George and Joyce, lover of Mexican food (I had a fact sheet on his vital stats; favorite color: blue). I found Brian on *Knots Landing,* where he played the son of the Machiavellian, shoulder-padded mommy Abby Cunningham. Abby was a horror show in heels and her daughter, Olivia, was a temperamental cokehead. In the middle of the exotic Californian dysfunction, there was Brian, sweet Brian, with the kindest, bluest eyes in the world, dapper in cornflower-blue matching pajamas, peaceful in sky-blue sweaters. Even when he got beat up because of his spiraling sister, he was handsome, black and blue. Oh, did my heart beat blue. I used to lie in bed and listen to Debbie Gibson's "Out of the Blue" and dream of Brian. I also thought it was pretty smart of me to find a guy on a prime-time soap that most people my age didn't watch. Brian was in *Tiger Beat* but he wasn't the Kirk Cameron level of famous. The odds were in my favor. I didn't want to be a fan. I wanted to be his girlfriend. I was going to be his girlfriend.

I picked up the first envelope, Brian's response to my fan outreach. Maybe it wouldn't be that bad. The envelope was brown and the handwriting was cursive, total eighties mom writing, swirly and dippy. I remember thinking it was cool that his mom wrote the envelope for him. To me, Brian was so famous that he didn't even have to write out his own envelopes. Wow, right?

Inside was a single sheet of small paper, the words typed. He addressed me by my first name (swoon) followed by a colon (sophisticated). He told me about a "pilot" called *Class of Beverly Hills* and oh that's right. I had forgotten about that tip, how cool I felt knowing about that show before anyone at school. Brian was so casual, so intimate. He opened up to me about his world philosophy regarding his departure from *Knots Landing:* "I won't say never, it always seems to make you look like an idiot when you say 'NEVER.'" Of course this letter lit me on fire. Here he was, waxing philosophical. And he was such a *nice* boy. He could have just talked about himself, but no. Brian talked about his mom. A lot. (This would become a recurring theme: How cool are moms?!) He said his mom wanted him to remind me that he was in an upcoming issue of *Soap Opera Digest.* But I thought this was so cool. He told her about me. She knows! His mom! Joyce Green! Joyce knows about me! It was all so real to me, it was the beginning of my life. My heart burst with bright blue ink, the color of his stamp. And that was before I saw *this,* sweet this: "How about sending a picture of yourself!!!!! Please!!! Thanks!"

Um, do you see all those fucking exclamation points??? I thought he wanted me so bad, oh yes. I know it doesn't make sense. Why did I think he was in love with me when he didn't even know what I looked like yet? But I believed it was possible. I had a job now: to make Brian Austin Green's dream come true, to send him a picture and make him fall in love with me. I had to sell myself to him, to prove that I alone could make him happy and go with him to Ed Debevic's. (Sidebar: Ed Debevic's was a diner in Beverly Hills where young Hollywood hung out. I was obsessed with it because I saw it in *Tiger Beat.* I was torn about what I wanted more: a night at Ed Debevic's with Brian and his famous friends, a night that would be photographed, printed in *Tiger Beat,* and passed around at my school, or a night at a school dance on the Cape so everyone at school could witness our love and realize that I was fucking amazing. This was the kind of shit I thought about. A lot.)

It would not be easy, making this hot Hollywood mama's

boy fall in love with me. And I had no idea that I was starring in the saddest romantic comedy ever, all by myself. No. I was blessed, tasked. I had to write the perfect letter. I had to be irresistible. I had to send him the right picture, the photograph that would make him get on a plane. I wasn't completely stupid. I knew that he wasn't fully sold on me yet. After all, he signed off, "Take care," and this was frustrating because of course when I first wrote to him I signed off *Love, Caroline.* As you might have figured out by now, I was not exactly the most popular girl in school, especially at this age. I was awkward, not in the way Charlize Theron says she was and you know she's exaggerating, that she just had glasses. No. I was truly awkward, not good at being me yet.

So I decided to create another Caroline, a sort of real-life Barbie doll that might be called the Better Than Me Girl. I thought it was romantic. Hey, isn't that supposed to be why we value true love, because it makes you want to be your best self? That's the twisted logic of seducing a famous actor via the United States Postal Service. I knew I didn't have to actually become cool and happy and popular. I only had to convince Brian that I was cool and happy and popular and then he would love me and the lie would become the truth. Oof. No wonder I hid these letters. I don't want to be someone who spent a summer trying to trick a television star into thinking I was cool, someone whose notion of love was wrapped up in revenge and celebrity and deception. I was not riding bikes with some boy next door like a "normal" girl. I was feverishly working on my fake identity. So when people ask if I'm anything like the deceitful guy I write stories about, well, it cannot be denied. Joe Goldberg lies to get love. In the summer of 1990, I did the same thing, minus the murder.

Obviously, I couldn't use any picture I already had. I needed something fresh, something cool and sexy. I had to look like the ultimate awesome chick. I chose a green-and-black paisley tank top from the Gap. (Reads: casually, totally not posing, just being pretty and stuff.) I asked my mom to buy film, at least two rolls. She did; she is a good mom. And when it was time for the shoot, I sat on the purple-and-blue sectional in our family room and twisted up like a pretzel. I wanted it to be candid, so I pretended to be talking and watching TV. I stroked my feathery hair and my noble mom advised me to maybe not do that. She told me to relax; I pretended to be Madonna in her "Express Yourself" video. She told me to be myself; I pretended to be Linda Evangelista in *Vogue*. Something else I was bad at besides making boys fall in love with me: modeling!

It goes without saying that I pitched a level-ten hissy fit when we got the pictures back at the mall. They were not good enough! I did not look like Madonna, damn it! My parents tried. My mom: "Stop being so hard on yourself. You look pretty." My dad: "You can be your own best friend or your own worst enemy. I like this one where you're laughing." But I wanted to be prettier than I was in those pictures; I wanted to look like the girl I was in my imagination, with glowing skin and soft hair and long legs. Those pictures were a lie and my imagination was the truth and I wanted to *kill* those pictures. This experience stayed with me. To this day, I don't like having my picture taken. Getting a photo for my book jacket was a nightmarish process with photographers pleading with me to relax. I do not like it now. I did not like it then.

That's where writing rescues me from the spiral of neurosis. I had to pick a picture because the clock was ticking and I had to finish my letter and I am happy to tell you that I felt the words I wrote to Brian mattered just as much, if not more, than my picture. The way I worked so hard to emanate sex appeal in front of the camera, I diligently crafted a Caroline that would jump off the page and into Brian's heart. I filled notebooks with variations on this potentially life-altering missive. I wrote and I rewrote and I would take a day off and then go back into it with fresh eyes. I was my own editor. And this was my big fiction even though I didn't know it at the time, not really.

The Caroline I invented was glamorous and wild, like Brian's cokehead sister on *Knots Landing*. I think I exaggerated about steal-ing flags on a golf course. I think I turned the flags into golf carts. I know I told him I drank. I remember using the word "booze" a lot. I told him that I was an *actress*. And this was bullshit. My brother and I had headshots and we had done extra work in some movies that were shot in Massachusetts. But I was not one of those homeschooled girls running around from audition to callback. I just wanted Brian and I to be equals. So that's kind of feminist, right? Anyway, I was obsessed with equality. The Better Than Me Caroline would be equal parts Glamorous Boozy Actress and Cute Cape Cod Girl. I wanted to be that girl who glams it up on the red carpet and then, boom, she's on a fishing boat. Fishing? Yeah. Fishing. I told Brian I love to go fishing. Which is a complete, total lie. Find me a twelve-year-old girl who does romantic algorithms in her pink and white diary and also enjoys dealing with bait. Not possible. She doesn't exist.

There was also an element of art. I experimented with dif-ferent handwriting styles, colored markers, pens. I deliberately spilled maple syrup on the paper to make it look like this was no big deal. But then I also wanted to seem funny so I circled the syrup with a magic marker. Fortunately, I did have some instincts and I didn't use that version. And eventually I sent the letter to Brian with one of the "natural" photos instead of the ones where I was pursing my lips in an attempt to ooze sex. (Thanks, Mom and Dad!) I went nuts waiting. Oh, I remember the wait. And then it was a miracle. Only a few weeks after I sent my fake heart and my real photo and my bullshit stories about boozing and fishing to Brian, he wrote back to me.

The main thing you have to know about his second letter: it was longer. It was an eight-by-ten sheet of paper. More is more. So before I read it, I believed that I had done it, that I made him fall in love with me. But the high wore off immediately. His opener was not the stuff of dreams: "First, thank you for the letter and especially the pic. I really like to see what 'fans' look like! It seems only fair, you know what I look like, right!!!"

I'm sure he thought he was being nice, but I wasn't looking for a discussion on the politics of identity and celebrity. I wanted a plane ticket. I wanted him to tell me I was beautiful. I remember being annoyed at him. Why was he calling me a fan? Why did he put the word "fan" in quotes? WTF was he thinking? Didn't he understand that I was not some stupid *fan*? Ugh. And he was so serious with me. He wished me a "happy and sane" Fourth of July. That bumped me. Sane? What kind of a teenage boy wants a girl to be *sane*? Why was he treating me like I was crazy? And then also, didn't boys *want* girls to be wild and crazy?

Things only got worse. Brian was thrilled to tell me that his pilot *Class of Beverly Hills* had been picked up. He acted like this was the best news in the world. He used the phrase "HOT OFF THE PRESS!!!!!!!" just like that, all caps, endearing, exuberant. He said he was stoked, and he put the word "stoked" in quotes. (Why the quotes? Why?) And I was not necessarily happy about any of this pilot business. He was supposed to be *mine*. I allowed myself to pursue him, in part, because he was not the Kirk Cameron level of famous. My friends didn't watch *Knots Landing*. Brian was both attractive and attainable to me. He was not the Joey McIntyre level of famous. I didn't want his star rising, the inevitable side effect of a show created for a teen audience. I was panicking and I was not even done reading the letter. It was about to get a hell of a lot worse: "Fishing—love it!! Last weekend, my mom, dad, Robin Thicke and I drove (5½ hours) to Mammoth. Robin and I went fishing, caught three beautiful trout, skinned, deboned and pan-fried them—how great!!!! Mammoth was the only vacation that I will have time to take this summer."

Every sentence was a machete.

Brian loves fishing, just like me. *I am a liar.*

Brian and his parents spent five hours in the car with a girl named Robin Thicke, aka the luckiest bitch in the world. *Robin is an evil bitch and Brian's parents love her.*

Brian is too busy for me. *He will not be surprising me, stepping off a jet, wearing Jams, and whisking me to the beach to show off in front of everyone.*

Oh, I was *fuming*. This came out of nowhere. He never said he had a girlfriend, let alone the kind of girlfriend who tags along on family fucking vacations. How dare that Robin Thicke bitch steal my man! Those active verbs he used: *skinned, deboned.* I just knew that after they pan-fried that fish they ate that fish and then after they ate that fish they kissed like fucking kissing fish. That's why he was using so many exclamation points. I was skinned. I was deboned. I had fucked it all up. And the dangerous thing about thinking it can get worse is that of course it can. Look at this next part: "Thanks for understanding about not giving out my personal home address and phone #."

AHAHAAAHAHAH. No, Caroline, no! I asked him for his phone number?! WTF was wrong with me? You don't ask a famous actor for his phone number! No, Caroline, noooooo! I wish I had better game. I wish I hadn't been so terminally aggressive. I feel like I might have scared him off, with good reason. Asking for his phone number is just wrong. You don't do that. No. Brian was changing. He was shifty. Look at this awkward shit he fed me to push me away: "When you (or if I say if you) join the fan club (I support it so there is no membership fee), they will keep you advised of what is the best address for you to write to me."

Is there anything worse than a boy you love being polite and detached? I was devastated to be downgraded. And if that wasn't bad enough, that fan shit, he'd also corrected me. He said he was not a "star" but just a "working actor." He was still the same sweet boy I fell in love with on *Knots* and I was still in it. Oh, he was so humble. Joyce did such a good job raising her son, so sweet, so shy. He signed off with his "Take care" and his peace sign and a peace sign is not a heart. But it's something. While the letter was typed, the signature was done by hand. It was his handwriting. His pen.

I wasn't gonna let that Robin Thicke bitch win. I wrote back to Brian, and I think I wrote back in a big way. I had to write my way back into his heart. I had to be better than his annoying big TV show and that Robin Thicke bitch. I am sure that I told him my acting career was just about to blow up. I probably retaliated and casually mentioned that I, too, was dating someone. I wanted to make him jealous, show him what he was missing. I didn't know it then, but this was my learning to deal with rejection and writing. I was fighting my way into Hollywood with my pen, just as I would years later.

Not to be dramatic or anything, but Brian's third and final letter to me is a revelation. It's an earthquake. I don't like it when people say something is "everything," but this letter, it is everything.

Smack in the middle of the page, no segue, no transition, the Greatest Two-Sentence Declaration of Gender by a Celebrity in the History of Two-Sentence Declarations of Gender by a Celebrity: "Robin is not a girl. Alan has two sons."

Okay, you knew that already but that's because it's twenty-five years later and you know Robin Thicke and his "Blurred Lines." This was 1990. He was just a kid back then and he wasn't famous and the best news of all was that he was a boy. A boy! Robin is a boy! *Yes!* Hallelujah! Relief! Rejoice! Brian didn't love me, but at least he didn't love Robin. I was free. I was stunned! Elated! Yes! It had never even occurred to me that Robin might be a boy. Joy! Praise Robin Thicke, son of Alan! I could breathe again. I could laugh; life was like an episode of *Three's Company* where it's just one mistaken identity after another. Robin is not a girl! I was so relieved.

And then, it's amusing now, twenty-five years later, that Robin Thicke is a household name, famous for singing a song called "Blurred Lines." Life is beautiful, right? *Robin is not a girl*. How the negative can be so positive. And also, we have to note the tone of this mini graph, the way the sentences are isolated. I read them now and think, *Imagine the crazy shit I wrote to this poor boy where he felt the need to clarify Robin's gender, as if this were a criminal deposition.* The absence of exclamation points is real. Hard-core.

Yep, everything was changing. In this letter, Brian was different. He told me that I was different, too. In the saddest little section at the bottom of the page, he promised me that his mom prioritizes "old fans" like me over "new fans." Ick, right? Who the fuck wants to be called an *old fan?* I know I didn't. But I also didn't care as much anymore. Robin Thicke was not a girl. I had driven myself crazy over nothing. And in some way, I wasn't obsessed with Brian anymore. I was backing off. I was cooling. I was going to be in *high school* and I was going to watch his show, but I do remember knowing that I was older now somehow, that I wasn't going to waste my time on this anymore.

And the thing about this letter, all of his letters, well, let's face it. Brian could be a little . . . strange. I didn't need some Hollywood boy telling me to be "sane" and I didn't like the way he was randomly putting stuff in quotes. And, you guys, not to be mean, but sometimes he sounded like a girl. For instance, in this letter he mentioned "Soleil Moon Frye's birthday bash." *Bash.* It's not really a teenage-boy kind of a word. None of the boys at school talked about going to *bashes.*

I also didn't know any boy who was so into gushing about his mother. Look at this Hallmarkian prose: "It never stops amazing me how, when you do something that they say is not smart, it turns out to be not such a smart idea! I think moms have a special gift or something!"

WTF was with this guy? Well, I didn't think about it anymore. I was over it. Crushes are everything until they are nothing. And with clear, calm, uninfatuated eyes, I can see things as they are, as they were. Let's be serious. I wasn't exchanging letters with Brian Austin Green. I think we all know that I was corresponding with another member of the Green family: Mrs. Joyce Green. Think about it. A mom would say all that stuff about mothers having a "special gift or something." I love that sentence if it comes from a stage mom who takes the time to deal with her son's lonely fans. And I also think it was cool of her to use this platform to remind girls to be good to their moms. It makes sense that Joyce was the one who called a party a "bash" and cushioned words like "stoked" and "set teacher" in quotation marks. She was quoting her son. She cared. She was honest in her deception. And obviously I have no right to be mad. After all, I wasn't me, either.

I can picture it, the way they worked together, Brian chilling out on a couch, playing with his Nintendo Game Boy. (I bet he got a free one when he did a commercial.) Joyce is at a table nearby, hunched over the typewriter.

"Honey!" she calls out. "Is it okay to say you're excited about the show?"

"Yep," he answers. "I'm stoked!"

Joyce lights up. *Stoked.* See, it works. And it's comforting to think that Brian and I were alike, with moms that were on our side, mine with her Nikon camera and her patience, Brian's with her typewriter and her L.A. slang. Yes, twenty-four years later, and I'm still compelled to find some common ground.

And it's endearing, the comedy of errors, my trying so hard to come off as this badass when all the while I was writing to his *mother.* If I had known, I would have created a completely different alter ego. I wouldn't have bragged about being a party girl. I would have made up some shit about rescuing a cat or babysitting. *I* would have been the one to say that I "hate to admit it" but moms rule. I can imagine how my letters must have disturbed Joyce. I picture her shaking her head.

"Honey," she says. "This poor girl, the one in Massachusetts, I don't know, Bri. She seems upset. She's asking about Robin. She's mad. Oh, honey, this is sad. I don't know what to do about this one."

Brian calls back: "Hold on, Mom!"

Joyce sighs, increasingly concerned about this girl from Cape Cod, the way she brags about drinking and stealing golf carts. Joyce can only hope that the girl is lying, that she has a mother who takes care of her. She is scared for her son sometimes, the way these girls write to him, obsess over him. She wishes she could hug all the fans, but she can't. What she can do: tell them to love their mothers. I sigh. Yes. I was writing with Brian's mom. Of course I was.

We are who we are. I like to invent voices. It's what I do in my writing. It's my drive in fiction. Back then I wanted to connect with Brian through a voice that was me, only not me, only me, only not me. And now I write from the perspective of a man who is me, only not me, only me, only not me. And it's my favorite thing in the world when someone reads my work and falls in love with the voice of the character. It's what I wanted from Brian. Also, I think fiction is a better outlet than fan mail.

When you're a kid, you think you're looking for love, you think you want your dreams to come true. But looking back on that summer, I know that I wasn't ready for anything real. Oh sure, I thought I was. I believed that if Brian showed up on the Cape, I would have instantly transformed into the Caroline who acted and fished and partied. I believed in the power of love. And I still believe in love.

And the one who really deserves a tribute is the almighty Joyce Green, the one who had to deal with all these girls who were trying to learn the difference between real life and fantasy. How exhausting it must have been, to read letters like mine, all the girls selling themselves, reaching, trying, screaming. It must have been so fucking loud, all of those misguided girls. I'm grateful for Joyce's exclamation points, her sensitivity, her disapproval of my party-girl persona. I just needed to try that voice out. It wasn't me. And I didn't really want Brian Austin Green showing up on Cape Cod. I only would have freaked out. I wasn't ready for anything real. Love does not transform you automatically. A crush makes you believe in it, but real love is like real change. It's slow. It's scary. It hurts.

Unless, of course, you're Hollywood hottie Brian Austin Green. I assumed my Brian was immune to rejection, standing on a pedestal with a million girls vying for his heart. So of course I was speechless when I saw the first couple of episodes of 90210. All this time, I thought of Brian as the super-cool god of Ed Debevic's and on 90210 he was playing the school *geek*. Was I stupid? Were they stupid? The world was upside down. Brian was David Silver, dorky and desperate, invading Kelly Taylor's space with his video camera, painfully insecure, human, salivating in pursuit of the cool kids, always one step behind, his clothes a little too bright and garish, reaching, running, posing. I was almost embarrassed because this meant that the guy I liked was actually a *nerd*. Brian was a human. I wondered if he had been embarrassed to tell me that he was playing the geek. Just as it never occurred to me that Robin Thicke was a boy, it had never seemed possible that the boy of my dreams was a geek. Of course I didn't idolize him anymore. I didn't idolize anyone.

My eye would soon wander to Brandon Walsh's good-boy jean jackets and Dylan McKay's bad-boy crinkly eyes, but I never wrote letters to Jason Priestley or Luke Perry. I wasn't naïve anymore. I was more interested in my real life. And I was confident. In the simplest way, Brian and I had had a conversation. I was proud of that. Hollywood boys didn't scare me. My freshman year of high school, my brother was an extra in the movie *School Ties*. I visited the set and watched then-unknown Ben Affleck and Matt Damon and Chris O'Donnell and I debated which one I would interview for my school paper. I picked Chris and we talked on the phone and I went on to interview celebrities for magazines as an adult.

I can tell you that adulthood agrees with Brian Austin Green. I know this because I see him sometimes. I've lived in L.A. for more than ten years, and it's a part of daily life, running into famous people. They really are *just like us*. They get coffee. You have to act normal and not stare. It's hard; you're in line waiting for your latte and Brian Austin Green is standing five feet away. Flesh, clothes, hair. You can almost smell him. My mind is always blown when we run into each other. (Sidebar: I am not a stalker. I am not the guy in my book. This is geography, luck; this is L.A. Yes, I know I am protesting too much. *Argh!*) I am "over him." But of course I still get butterflies when I bump into him.

I still think he's probably one of the sweetest, hottest guys in the world. There's something rare about him. He has a genuinely happy resting face. His eyes smile even when he's just standing there, doing nothing. He seems like a really great, present father. Sometimes he has his baby and that baby looks *happy*. Brian Austin Green beams in a way that a lot of people in L.A. do not, particularly actors. I love crossing paths with him. It's always a quiet moment of joy, standing nearby my cornflower-blue crush. He's so tall, so grown-up, so buff, so tattooed. I am always tempted to approach him, to reminisce about our long-distance summer together, to thank Joyce for her kind, thoughtful words. My heart palpitates when our eyes meet for a nanosecond and it becomes possible for me to say something, start something. "Excuse me, Brian," I would begin. "This will sound crazy, but I used to write to you when I was a kid."

I imagine what would happen next. We would laugh about the past and I would talk too fast, say too much about how excited I was every time I tore into those letters, how good it felt to believe that Brian Austin Green was writing to me, just me, to tell me that moms have "a special gift or something." But I never do start the conversation. Instead, I bite my lip. I look away. The thing is, if we started talking, it would change everything. And I'd probably feel compelled to ask for a picture and of course the picture would never be good enough. Brian never hangs around the coffee shop. He always leaves when his order comes through. I stay and catch my breath. I feel like I won, like I kept the dynamic in place. I preserved a little piece of my young, hungry heart.

EMILY GOULD

My So-Called Crush on Jared Leto

The other day I was walking in SoHo and caught a glimpse of a former crush. More specifically: I had stepped out of pedestrian traffic onto a stoop in order to send an urgent tweet about how well I'd just spent a $100 Dean & DeLuca gift certificate and I saw this former crush entering the Equinox gym a few doors down. The sighting was probably 2.5 seconds long and I was still reeling from my hallucinatory detour into the world of $22 jam, so I didn't have time to assimilate a lot of information. It was definitely him, though, and he looked mostly the same—skin rougher and ruddier, hair unbecomingly puffed by the day's humidity, but not fat or bald or otherwise overtly bad. Still, though, a complex cocktail of emotions made its way through my limbic system as I continued down Spring Street. First there was the faintest, tiniest hint of the way I'd once felt about him—the way seeing his face on the street would have made me feel during the period when this unlikely dude had been the subject of all my thoughts. Almost immediately, though, that faint rush was overwhelmed by a much larger dose of palm-prickling, skin-flushing embarrassment, shading into existential horror. Who had felt that way about him? I had? Me? *Him?*

I bring this up because this is also how I feel every time I turn a magazine page or click open a new tab and see Jared Leto.

Jared Leto is a preternaturally slender and "youthful" forty-three-year-old with, let's all be honest with ourselves about this, a lot of Botox or fillers or *something* going on in the eye area that makes him look stretched and overly awake. He has for years been the front man of a band with the terrible, terrible name Thirty Seconds to Mars. He's been in movies, some of them good. But mostly, he's known for being Jared Leto—for dating models, wearing stupid outfits, having ombré highlights, and being a "rock star" whose music, I guess, has "fans," in some kind of alternate-universe L.A. way where the idea of being a musician or an actor is often more important than making music or acting. He has a publicist who gets him into *Us Weekly* on a regular basis, even if it's just into the column on the left-hand side of the page where births and deaths are announced that features obviously publicist-placed "sightings" of celebrities drinking specific brands of tequila.

But back in 1994, he was Jordan Catalano, the crush object of the narrator of *My So-Called Life*. This hour-long drama aired on ABC for one season and is still the best fictional representation of being a fourteen-year-old girl that has ever existed, and it came into existence just in time for me to be the perfect age to appreciate it. Paeans to the glory of *MSCL* exist in abundance, so I'll spare you. More to the point here, Jared/Jordan's was the first on-screen presence ever to make teenage me feel overwhelmed by longing. Before him, I'd only pretended to understand what my peers were talking about when they described their feelings for members of the New Kids on the Block or, later, Weezer. I had sort of thought I wasn't someone who "got" crushes, at least not on celebrities. What could be the point of being into someone who could never reciprocate, or even know you were alive, someone who not only didn't go to your school but didn't even live in the same city or state or, functionally speaking, universe? But I caught my first glimpse of—can we just call him Jordan?—and finally, I got it.

It wasn't only that Jordan was beautiful, though of course he was—shaggy haired, baby faced, with perfect ice-blue eyes and cherubic, kiss-demanding lips and a tantalizingly unrevealed body.

Grunge-era fashion was ideal for my particular stage of sexual development; tight pants and muscle tees would have been too overt, too frankly sexual for me at that time. At thirteen, you don't actually want that much information. Better, then, was a style like Jordan's: layers of flannel over layers of waffle-weave thermals over layers of T-shirt. A body was under there, probably! You could think about it, or not, as much as you wanted to, without ever being confronted with its nonnegotiable reality.

The trick of Jordan's appeal, though, and what set him apart from other perfect-lipped, flannel-draped heartthrobs of his era, was his personality. Or rather, his lack thereof. The best thing about Jordan was how he existed almost exclusively in narrator Angela Chase's fervid imagination. In the rare moments that he did ever speak, or otherwise betray any kind of interiority or life independent from the life he lived in Angela's fantasies, you mostly just wanted him to shut up. With every mumbled sentence fragment, he threatened to disrupt the image Angela (and, by extension, I) had constructed of him. Jordan was quiet, moody, bad at reading (vulnerable! needy!). The actual Jordan was probably other things, too, and the show was sophisticated enough to hint at these: A little bit dumb, maybe. A little bit sexually opportunistic—he eventually has sex with Angela's best friend, Rayanne, for no better reason than she is drunk and willing to have sex with him. A lot uninvested in Angela, or in having anything like a real relationship with her. Like a lot of boys—like all teenage boys, really—his real self was much less interesting than anything you could imagine him to be. But you could imagine him to be anything. Also, he seemed to be fantastic at kissing. And at leaning. "Don't you love the way he leans?" Angela memorably sighs to her gay friend Rickie. That someone could have a talent for leaning in a compelling way—the idea that leaning could be compelling—these were new, newly relevant concepts for me. I started to look around my own school for good leaners.

It's not altogether surprising that a crush based on a second-hand experience of a crush—in other words, my crush on Jared, which was really just an imitation of fictional Angela's on fictional Jordan—would be intense but finite. But if I learned how to have a crush from Angela, I learned how to stop having one from my experience with Jared. I learned from wanting and then opposite-of-wanting him that it was not just possible but likely that when a crush or an affair had run its course, you could feel an inescapable wave of nausea where once the pull of attraction had been just as automatic and just as strong. This was the lesson of Jared/Jordan, and though it never made me do anything differently, it did prepare me psychologically for the possibility that lust could turn into revulsion as surely as delicious cake turns into decaying garbage if you leave it in the back of the fridge too long.

Jared recently dyed his hair an icy blond. He seems to be emulating Tilda Swinton sartorially, or maybe Karl Lagerfeld. God bless him. I hope he's having fun. I would sooner make out with any other living *MSCL* cast member, including the actors who played Angela's parents, Graham and Patty, than bestow one closed-mouthed kiss on Jared Leto now. But if I could be transported back in time to his prime, I wouldn't hesitate. Especially if we could make out in the boiler room.

A final look at what happens when celebrity crushes play out in the real world.

CAROLYN PARKHURST

Celebrity Fantasies and Their Logical Conclusions

Through a series of surprisingly believable coincidences, you meet Jon Hamm at a party. There's an immediate spark; you both feel it, and soon, the two of you are having frequent and enthusiastic sex. You become intimately familiar with the magnificent landscape that is Jon Hamm's body. You regale your friends with stories about the way you and Jon Hamm have pleasured each other in limos and elevators and backstage at the Emmy Awards. You send him filthy texts in the greenroom of *Good Morning America*. In this manner, several years pass.

At some point, you notice that you and Jon Hamm spend your evenings sitting in the same room with your own individual laptops, barely talking at all. Sometimes you find yourself sending Jon Hamm an e-mail about something funny that you read, even though he's in *the same freaking room*. One time, you actually text Jon Hamm from upstairs to ask him to bring you a glass of wine; you're not even that surprised when he refuses. You still really like each other and everything—and, hey, he's still Jon Hamm. It's just that right now, you're really busy reading this one thing on Facebook, and it's just not a good time to talk. It doesn't matter, right? You and Jon Hamm will have sex and a conversation tomorrow.

*　　*　　*

Hugh Jackman provides a refreshing change of pace. He's such a skilled actor that role-playing scenarios don't feel ridiculous at all. He *is* Wolverine, and he makes you believe that you're . . . whoever, that chick with the mind-control powers.

It's not a surprise to learn that you're not the only one with whom Hugh Jackman is sharing his considerable talents. You don't mind; you are, after all, still seeing Jon Hamm. But the scheduling becomes more and more difficult, and soon you realize that he's not making much of an effort to slot you in. You agree to a couple of "double bookings," but eventually that dries up, too. After a while, you're not even invited to watch.

On a weekend trip to Las Vegas, you're approached at the roulette table by a man who looks familiar, though it takes you a minute to place him.

"Shaun Cassidy," he says, saving you both the embarrassment.

"Right," you say. "Of course." You hold out your hand, which he clasps between both of his.

He looks into your eyes; his expression is earnest and hopeful. "I'm here on behalf of . . . well, there's a group of us that have gotten together . . ." He gestures over his shoulder and you notice that a small cluster of men have gathered behind him and are watching your conversation with some interest. Among them, you spot Emilio Estevez, Billy Idol, and Ricky Schroder. (Sorry, "Rick.")

"Um," you say.

"We have a proposition for you," says Shaun. "We'll pay you a million dollars . . ."

Behind him, there's some jostling, and someone clears his throat.

"Uh, just a minute," says Shaun. The men confer in whispers, then Shaun turns back to you. "Nine hundred thousand," he says. "We'll pay you nine hundred thousand dollars for one night together."

Your eyes narrow. "I don't . . . ," you begin. "Wait, all of you?"

"Well," says Shaun, "only if that's a . . . thing for you. Really, the details are up to you."

You look them over, considering. It's tempting, kind of.

"You couldn't get Bowie?" you ask.

Shaun shakes his head. "Nope. He's sixty-eight, happily married, and still way out of your league."

You nod. You figured as much. Still, it's not a bad group. There's Andrew McCarthy. There's Jake from *Sixteen Candles* and that one guy from Depeche Mode. But you're in the middle of a lucky streak, gambling-wise, and you have plans to meet up with some friends in half an hour.

"That's very generous," you begin, "but I'm afraid I'm going to have to decline."

They take it well; they don't seem particularly surprised. There are hugs all around, and as they walk away, you're pretty sure you've made the right decision. They've probably got better ways to spend their money. And none of you are the same people you used to be.

Johnny Depp turns out to be good company, as well as a skilled practitioner in both erotic and nonerotic massage. He displays a surprising breadth of knowledge about . . . blah blah blah, something with handcuffs, it's a revelation, and so forth.

The first time he calls in the middle of the night, it's to ask what you meant when you described his acting style as "idiosyncratic." The second time, it's to tell you that the episode of *SpongeBob* he guest-starred on is showing on Nick. Soon you find that you're spending more time as a film critic than as a sex toy. The day you admit that you never saw the third *Pirates of the Caribbean* movie and don't intend to is the beginning of the end.

Later, couching your language in hypotheticals, you share your bewilderment with a friend. Why is there always such a mismatch between expectation and reality? She just laughs. "What, you really thought it would never get stale? Talk to me when you've been together as long as me and George Clooney."

About the Authors

Cathy Alter is a popular author and writer whose feature articles, essays, and reviews have appeared in local and national newspapers and magazines including the *New York Times,* the *Washington Post, Washingtonian,* TheAtlantic.com, the *Huffington Post, Arlington Magazine,* the New York *Daily News, Self, McSweeney's, Smith Magazine* and Six-Word Memoir, *Urbanite,* and the *Washington City Paper.*

Her book *Virgin Territory: Stories from the Road to Womanhood* was released in 2004 and her memoir, *Up for Renewal: What Magazines Taught Me About Love, Sex, and Starting Over,* was released in July 2008.

She has appeared on television and radio programs such as the *Today* show and NPR. She has been a frequent panelist for organizations including Fall for the Book, American Independent Writers, the Baltimore Writers' Conference, the Gaithersburg Book

Festival, the F. Scott Fitzgerald Literary Conference, the Bethesda Literary Festival, and Conversations and Connections.

Cathy received a BA from Colgate University and an MA from Johns Hopkins University. She lives in Washington, DC, with her husband and son.

Dave Singleton is an award-winning writer/producer, memoir and creative nonfiction teacher, and multimedia communications editor. He currently writes for numerous publications and websites on a variety of topics, including pop culture, food, travel, social trends, dating and relationships, LGBT life, and health and caregiving.

He's the author of two books: *The Mandates: 25 Real Rules for Successful Gay Dating* and *Behind Every Great Woman There's a Fabulous Gay Man: Advice from a Guy Who Gives It to You Straight.*

He's been a columnist for Caring.com since 2012 and, since 2003, has written regularly for Match.com, Yahoo!, AOL, and MSN on dating and relationships, for all audiences: gay and straight, men and women, younger and older, and from all backgrounds. The total readership number for his Yahoo! and Match *Happen* magazine columns since 2011 has reached over 22 million.

He has appeared on television and radio programs for NBC News, NPR, the BBC, and AARP's *Prime Time Focus.* His work has been featured in numerous print and online media outlets such as the *Washington Post, National Journal,* the *Chicago Tribune, Washingtonian,* PBS, *AARP The Magazine* and AARP Media, the *Arizona Republic,* the UK *Sun,* the *Sydney Morning Herald, Happen, Cosmopolitan, Glamour, Elle, Harper's Bazaar, Tango, Metro Weekly, Instinct, Attitude,* and *Out.*

For the twenty-two-part multimedia (print, online, radio, and TV) report on the Stonewall Riots' fortieth anniversary for AARP Media, he received national awards in 2010: a MIN (Media Industry News) Award for Outstanding Exclusive Coverage; a GLAAD Media Award for Outstanding Multimedia Journalism; and an NLGJA

(National Lesbian and Gay Journalists Association) Excellence in Journalism Award. He received the second-place 2015 NLGJA Excellence in Online Journalism Award for "Finding Pride and Home: A Look at Housing for Older LGBT Adults," published by Caring.com.

He teaches creative nonfiction and memoir at the Writer's Center in Bethesda, Maryland, and speaks at colleges, conferences, and events. A graduate of the University of Virginia and New York University, he currently resides in Washington, DC.

Contributor Biographies

Amin Ahmad was raised in India and educated at Vassar College and MIT. His essays and stories have been published in literary magazines and listed in *The Best American Essays*. As A. X. Ahmad, he is the author of the suspense novels *The Caretaker* and *The Last Taxi Ride*. He teaches creative writing at the Writer's Center in Bethesda, Maryland.

Jessica Anya Blau is a novelist whose newest novel, *The Wonder Bread Summer,* was picked for CNN's summer reading list, NPR's summer reading list, *Vanity Fair's* summer reads, and Oprah's Book Club's summer reading list. Her novel *Drinking Closer to Home* was featured in Target stores as a "Breakout Book" and made many lists of the best books of the year. Jessica's first novel, *The Summer of Naked Swim Parties,* was a national bestseller and was picked as a Best Summer Book by the *Today* show, the *New York Post,* and *New York Magazine*. The *San Francisco Chronicle* and other newspapers chose it as one of the best books of the year. *The Summer of Naked Swim Parties* and *The Wonder Bread Summer* have both been optioned for film and are currently in preproduction. Jessica cowrote the screenplay for the film *Love on the Run,* which is currently in postproduction. Her fourth novel, *The Trouble with Lexie,* will be out in the summer of 2016.

Michelle Brafman is the author of *We Named Them All: Stories* and the novel *Washing the Dead*. Her writing has appeared in *Slate, Tablet,* the *Washington Post,* and elsewhere. She teaches fiction writing at the Johns Hopkins University MA in Writing Program.

Anna Breslaw has written for the *New York Times,* Jezebel, *Cosmopolitan, New York Magazine, The Cut,* and elsewhere. Her debut young adult novel, *Scarlett Epstein Hates It Here,* was published in April 2016. She lives in New York.

Jamie Brisick is the author of *Becoming Westerly: Surf Champion Peter Drouyn's Transformation into Westerly Windina; Have Board, Will Travel: The Definitive History of Surf, Skate, and Snow;* and *We Approach Our Martinis with Such High Expectations.* He is presently global editor of *Huck.* He was previously executive editor of *Surfing.* His journalism has appeared in the *New York Times, Details,* the *Guardian,* and the *Sydney Morning Herald.* In 2008 he was awarded a Fulbright Scholarship to study and write about youth culture in Japan. He lives in Los Angeles.

Yesha Callahan is a writer currently based in the DC area. Since 2007, Yesha has brought her unique sense of humor to subjects ranging from dating to trending topics, entertainment, and black culture on her website. In addition to her own site, Yesha has also written for *Clutch Magazine, Jezebel, The Grio,* and BlogHer, and is currently a staff writer for *The Root.* Yesha was also a comedy and politics writer for BET's late-night talk show *Don't Sleep!,* hosted by former CNN anchor T. J. Holmes, and is currently working with *The Daily Show*'s cocreator Madeleine Smithberg on several TV projects.

Shulem Deen is the author of All Who Go Do Not Return, a memoir about growing up in and then leaving the Hasidic Jewish world. His work has appeared in The New Republic, Salon, Tablet Magazine, and The Forward, among others, and in 2015 he was listed in the Forward 50, an annual list of American Jews with outsized roles on political and social issues. He serves as a board member at Footsteps, a New York City–based organization that offers assistance and support to those who have left the ultra-Orthodox Jewish community. He lives in Brooklyn, New York.

Jason Diamond is the author of the memoir *Searching for John Hughes* (William Morrow, 2016), the founder of *Vol. 1 Brooklyn,* and an associate editor at *Men's Journal.* He lives in Brooklyn with his wife, two cats, and a dog named Max.

Larry Doyle paid good money for a website called LarryDoyle.com, thus trivializing the other 261 Larry Doyles in the country. Or you could Google him. He's not the chef, the sheriff, or the Wall Street jerk. And he also didn't play second base for the New York Giants from 1907 to 1920.

James Franco is an actor, director, screenwriter, producer, teacher, and author. He began his career on *Freaks and Geeks* and received a Golden Globe Award for his performance in the biographical film *James Dean.* Notable film credits include *Oz the Great and Powerful, Spring Breakers,* the *Spider-Man* trilogy, *Milk,* and *127 Hours,* for which he received Academy Award, SAG, and Golden Globe nominations for Best Actor. He has directed, written, and produced several features and has been published several times in magazines and through his own books. He is currently teaching college courses at UCLA, USC, and CalArts, and acting classes at Studio 4, and recently made his Broadway debut in *Of Mice and Men,* to rave reviews.

Roxane Gay's writing has appeared or is forthcoming in *Best American Mystery Stories 2014, Best American Short Stories 2012, Best Sex Writing 2012, A Public Space, McSweeney's, Tin House, Oxford American, American Short Fiction, West Branch, Virginia Quarterly Review, NOON,* the *New York Times Book Review, Bookforum, Time,* the *Los Angeles Times, The Nation, The Rumpus, Salon,* and many others. She is the coeditor of *PANK.* She is also the author of the books *Ayiti, An Untamed State, Bad Feminist,* and *Hunger,* forthcoming from HarperCollins in 2016.

Emily Gould is the author of *Friendship* and *And the Heart Says Whatever* and the co-owner of a feminist publishing start-up, Emily Books, which sells new and backlist titles via a subscription model.

Barbara Graham is an author, essayist, journalist, and playwright. Her essays and articles have appeared in many magazines, including *Glamour; More; National Geographic Traveler; O, The Oprah Magazine; Psychotherapy Networker; Redbook; Self; Shambhala Sun; Time; Tricycle; Utne Reader;* and *Vogue,* and have been collected in numerous anthologies. She has written for websites hosted by AARP, Babble, Beliefnet, Grandparents.com, *The Huffington Post,* NPR, WowOWow, and PurpleClover.com. She is the author/editor of the *New York Times* bestseller *Eye of My Heart: 27 Women Writers Reveal the Hidden Pleasures and Perils of Being a Grandmother* and author of *Women Who Run with the Poodles: Myths and Tips for Honoring Your Mood Swings.* Barbara's plays have been produced Off-Broadway and at theaters around the country. Her most recent book is *Camp Paradox.*

Shane Harris is an author and journalist who has written extensively about intelligence and national security. His new book, *@War: The Rise of the Military-Internet Complex* (Eamon Dolan/ Houghton Mifflin Harcourt, 2014), explores the front lines of America's new cyber war. Shane's first book, *The Watchers* (Penguin Press, 2010), tells the story of five men who played central roles in the creation of a vast national security apparatus and the rise of surveillance in America. *The Watchers* won the New York Public Library's Helen Bernstein Book Award for Excellence in Journalism, and the *Economist* named it one of the best books of 2010. Shane is the winner of the 2010 Gerald R. Ford Prize for Distinguished Reporting on National Defense. He is currently a senior correspondent at the *Daily Beast.* His work has appeared in the *New York Times,* the *Wall Street Journal, Slate,* TheAtlantic.com, and the *Washington Post.*

Dave Housley's third collection of short fiction, *If I Knew the Way, I Would Take You Home,* was published by Dzanc Books in January 2015. He is also the author of *Commercial Fiction* (Outpost 19), a book of short stories based on television commercials, and

Ryan Seacrest Is Famous (Impetus Press; Dzanc Books eBook Reprint). He is one of the founding editors of *Barrelhouse* magazine and a cofounder of the Conversations and Connections writers' conference. Sometimes he drinks boxed wine and tweets about the things on his television at @housleydave.

Jill Kargman is a *New York Times* bestselling author and the creator and star of *Odd Mom Out,* Bravo's first scripted comedy. She lives in New York City with her husband and three children.

David Keplinger is the author of four collections of poetry, most recently *The Most Natural Thing.* For his work he's been awarded the Cavafy Poetry Prize; the T. S. Eliot Prize, selected by Mary Oliver; the Colorado Book Award; and a fellowship from the National Endowment for the Arts.

Caroline Kepnes holds a bachelor of arts degree in American civilization from Brown University. She started out her journalism career as the associate editor of both *Tiger Beat* and *Teen Machine.* Her favorite part of the job was reading the handwritten letters from fans. Caroline is a novelist now, the author of *You* and *Hidden Bodies. You* was optioned by Showtime and has been translated into seventeen languages. She splits her time between Los Angeles, California, and Cape Cod, Massachusetts.

Stephen King was born in Portland, Maine, in 1947, the second son of Donald and Nellie Ruth Pillsbury King. He made his first professional short story sale in 1967 to *Startling Mystery Stories.* In the fall of 1971, he began teaching high school English classes at Hampden Academy, the public high school in Hampden, Maine. Writing in the evenings and on the weekends, he continued to produce short stories and to work on novels. In the spring of 1973, Doubleday & Co. accepted the novel *Carrie* for publication, providing him the means to leave teaching and write full-time. He has since published over fifty books and has become one of the world's most successful writers. Stephen lives in Maine and Florida with his wife, novelist Tabitha King. They are regular contributors to a number of charities, including many libraries, and have been honored locally for their philanthropic activities.

Richard McCann holds an MA in creative writing and modern literature from Hollins University and a PhD in American studies from the University of Iowa. The author of the story collection *Mother of Sorrows* and the poetry collection *Ghost Letters,* McCann's writing has appeared in the *Atlantic, Esquire, Tin House,* and elsewhere. He has received fellowships from the Guggenheim Foundation, the National Endowment for the Arts, and the Fine Arts Work Center in Provincetown, on whose board of trustees he served from 2000 to 2008. He teaches in the MFA program in creative writing at American University.

Andrew McCarthy is an actor, director, and award-winning travel writer. He has appeared in dozens of films, including *Pretty in Pink* (which made him the joyful recipient of numerous first crushes). Andrew is an editor at large at *National Geographic Traveler,* and his travel memoir, *The Longest Way Home,* became a *New York Times* bestseller.

Kermit Moyer is an emeritus professor of literature and creative writing from American University in Washington, DC, where he taught for thirty-seven years before moving with his wife, Amy, to Cape Cod in 2007. He is the author of *Tumbling* (University of Illinois Press), a collection of short stories that was called "impeccable" by the *New York Times Book Review,* and *The Chester Chronicles* (the Permanent Press), a novel-in-stories that won the 2011 L. L. Winship PEN/New England Award in Fiction.

Kimberly Dawn Neumann is the coauthor of two books: *The Real Reasons Men Commit: Why He Will—or Won't—Love, Honor, and Marry You,* and *Sex Comes First: 15 Ways to Save Your Relationship . . . Without Leaving Your Bedroom.* Her work has appeared in such publications as *Cosmopolitan, Marie Claire, Real Simple, Women's Health,* and *Redbook,* and in numerous online publications. She was a columnist at Match.com with Dave Singleton for over ten years. A summa cum laude graduate from the University of Maryland Philip Merrill College of Journalism, she's also a performer who has appeared on Broadway in *A Chorus Line, Ragtime, Urban Cowboy,* and *Annie Get Your Gun,* as well as in many national tours, Off-Broadway shows, and also TV and film. Visit her website at KDNeumann.com.

Carolyn Parkhurst is the *New York Times* bestselling author of three novels (*The Dogs of Babel, Lost and Found,* and *The Nobodies Album*) and a children's picture book. She lives in Washington, DC, with her husband and two children. Her fourth novel, *Harmony,* will be published in 2017 by Pamela Dorman Books.

Jodi Picoult is the bestselling author of twenty-three books, the last eight of which, including her most recent novel, *Leaving Time,* have debuted at number one on the *New York Times* bestseller list. Over 40 million of her books are in print, and several have been adapted for TV and screen. She is also the coauthor, along with her daughter Samantha van Leer, of a YA series, which is currently being adapted as a Broadway musical.

Julia Pierpont is the author of *Among the Ten Thousand Things,* her debut novel. She is a graduate of Barnard College and the MFA program at NYU, where she was a Rona Jaffe Graduate Fellow, as well as the recipient of a Stein Fellowship. She works at *The New Yorker* and lives in Brooklyn with her lunatic dog, Dash.

Joanna Rakoff is the author of the novel *A Fortunate Age* and the bestselling memoir *My Salinger Year.* She lives in Cambridge, Massachusetts, with her husband and children.

Hanna Rosin is a writer for the *Atlantic* and *Slate,* and author of *The End of Men.* In 2009 she was nominated for a National Magazine Award for her *Atlantic* story about transgendered children, "A Boy's Life." In 2010 she won the award as part of a package of stories in *New York* magazine about circumcision. Lately, she's been writing a lot about crime—murder, attempted murder, sexting (which is, in fact, a crime). In 2010, Rosin headlined the first TED women's conference, held in Washington, DC. She has appeared on *The Daily Show with Jon Stewart* and *The Colbert Report*. She lives in Washington, DC, with her husband, David Plotz, her daughter, and her two sons.

Janice Shapiro is the author of *Bummer and Other Stories* (Soft Skull Press, 2010). Her stories and comics have been published in many publications, including the *North American Review,* the *Santa Monica Review, Fifty-Two Stories, Storyville,* and the *Seattle Review.* Her weekly comic, *Size 8,* appears in the online literary magazine *Real Pants.* She is at work on a graphic memoir, *Crushable: My Life in Crushes from Ricky Nelson to Viggo Mortensen.*

David Shields is the international bestselling author of twenty books, including *Reality Hunger* (named one of the best books of 2010 by more than thirty publications), *The Thing About Life Is That One Day You'll Be Dead* (*New York Times* bestseller), and *Black Planet* (finalist for the National Book Critics Circle Award). Forthcoming are *War Is Beautiful* (powerHouse), *Flip-Side* (powerHouse, 2016) and *Other People* (Knopf, 2017). The recipient of Guggenheim and NEA fellowships, Shields has published essays and stories in the *New York Times Magazine, Harper's, Esquire, Yale Review,* the *Village Voice, Salon, Slate, McSweeney's,* and the *Believer.* His work has been translated into twenty languages.

Larry Smith is a writer and the founder of *Smith Magazine,* the launchpad of Six-Word Memoirs, the bestselling book series based on this simple challenge: Can you tell your life story in six words? Larry has led workshops on storytelling with teams at Intuit, Levi's, Dell, Shutterfly, and ESPN, and at schools across the country. He once finished second in a demolition derby race. Visit www.sixwordmemoirs.com/larrysmith.

Karin Tanabe is the author of *The Price of Inheritance, The List,* and the forthcoming *The Gilded Years.* A former *Politico* reporter, her writing has appeared in the *Chicago Tribune,* the *Miami Herald,* and the *Washington Post,* among other publications. She lives in Washington, DC.

Tony Tulathimutte is the author of the novel *Private Citizens* and has contributed fiction and essays to *Threepenny Review, AGNI, Vice, The New Yorker* online, *Salon,* and elsewhere. A graduate of Stanford University and the Iowa Writers' Workshop, he has received an O. Henry Award, a MacDowell Fellowship, and the Michener-Copernicus Society of America Award. He lives in New York.

Sam Weisman gave up his dream to become the shortest Jewish player in the NBA for a career in the entertainment business. He is a graduate of Deerfield Academy and Yale University (BA in music history), and earned an MFA in acting and directing at Brandeis University.

After making a living as an actor for ten years, Sam started directing, working in theater, television, and film. His TV credits include *Family Ties, Moonlighting, L.A. Law, Brooklyn Bridge,* and the pilot of *7th Heaven.* His films include *D2: The Mighty Ducks, George of the Jungle,* and *Dickie Roberts: Former Child Star.*

As cocreator and executive producer of the a cappella music competition show *The Sing-Off,* Sam was instrumental in bringing all-vocal music into mainstream pop culture in recent years, helping to launch the career of Pentatonix.

Sam is most proud of his children, Marguerite and Dan. He lives with his wife, Constance McCashin, in the Boston area, and is a die-hard sports fan.

Marion Winik's books include the memoir *First Comes Love* (1996), a *New York Times* Notable Book, and the cult classic *The Glen Rock Book of the Dead,* the book Cheryl Strayed said she most often recommends to other people. She writes a monthly column at BaltimoreFishbowl.com, reviews books for *Newsday* and Kirkus, and is a longtime NPR commentator. She lives in Baltimore with her teenage daughter and teaches in the MFA program at the University of Baltimore. Find more information and links at MarionWinik.com.

Nicola Yoon is the number one *New York Times* bestselling author of *Everything, Everything*. Originally from Jamaica (the island) and Brooklyn (part of Long Island), she currently resides in Los Angeles, California, with her husband and daughter, both of whom she loves beyond all reason.

Acknowledgments

From Cathy

It must be said: This book would not exist if not for the brilliance of Dave, my friend, coconspirator, and forever the Snazz to my Razz.

There is so much more to be said about the process that produced this book, but for now I wish to express my profound gratitude to Wendy Sherman and everyone at Wendy Sherman & Associates. Also to Kim Curtin, the first leg in the long journey toward publication. Big thanks go to the supremely smart and dynamic team at HarperCollins, including the delightfulness of Margaux Weisman, Katherine Nintzel, Jessie Edwards, Kaitlin Harri, Ivy McFadden, and Jeanne Reina. We're so lucky to have you in our corner.

Next, to my father, Elliott, who proudly pointed out Blythe Danner in Rizzoli Bookstore but spectacularly failed to recognize Susan Sarandon a few minutes later. To my brother, David, who happily trailed Steve Martin around Barneys with me. And to my cousin Stephanie, for getting me a signed photo of Ron Jeremy, which still needs a good frame.

To my valued friends Maria Streshinsky, Annie Groer, and Billy Fox, who weighed in constantly with advice, wisdom, and word choice. To Barbara Martin, Jayne Sandman, and Jackie Leventhal, for knowing anyone who's someone. And to my sidekick, Patti Anderson, who offered her counsel and level head.

Of course to my husband, Karl, who knows that although writing does not entail much heavy lifting, there is nevertheless a great burden in words. And to our boy, Leo, who, at four, is still blissfully unaware of celebrity. For now.

Finally, to all our contributors, who gave us so much for so little.

From Dave

Sometimes you labor over what to do next. It's a painstaking process of fidgeting, researching, and strategizing. In the case of this book, it was two old friends reunited, drinking Manhattans and deciding in a split second to collaborate. It took us all of ten minutes to consider what would be fun both to write *and* read, followed by glasses clinking and two voices in resounding unison saying, "Hell yes." Thank you *times a million* to dazzling Razz, aka Cathy, for never wavering once as we stuck together through thick and thin to see our vision come to life.

Thank you to persevering Kim Perel and Wendy Sherman, who always believed in this book, represented us well, and reassured us that connecting writers to the right publisher is like dating: "It only takes one to find the right match."

They were right. It was love at first sight meeting our Harper-Collins editor, Margaux Weisman. Thank you, Margaux, for all you've done to make our experience a start-to-finish delight. How lucky we are to have such a talented and dedicated *CRUSH* publishing team, including Katherine Nintzel, Jessie Edwards, Kaitlin Harri, Ivy McFadden, and Jeanne Reina.

Thank you to my family and friends for supporting this book, especially those who provided excellent ideas, much-needed inspiration, and infectious enthusiasm: Gail Ross, Peter Hass, Kit Moyer, Amy Gussack, Dori Sless, David Sless, David Keplinger, Richard McCann, Kimberly Dawn Neumann, Beau Singleton, Bruce Singleton, Amy Singleton, Kaya Singleton, Shane Harris, Christopher Kerns, Gaby Zabalua, Nina Halper, Jon Dauphine, Thom Martin, Abby Miller, Leslie Goldman, Bruce Morman, Patrick Sammon, Daniel Denecke, Lisa Blake, Ava Seave, John Stoltenberg, Patricia Davis, Mark Bradbury, Vic Lemas, Sacha Millstone, Sarah Brezniak, Jen Mowad, Jessica Gessner, Kelly Zacchini, Eric Brahney, Hugh Delehanty, Barbara Graham, the "Fab Six," and my colleagues and students at The Writer's Center.

A smiling hat tip to the naysayers who said, "No one buys anthologies," "Who cares about crushes?," "This only works if Lady Gaga writes about Madonna," and other supportive statements like that. You taught me that *no* means, at various times, *maybe, not now, I have no idea, no one else ever did this so . . no, what does everyone else think?*, and, eventually, *yes!*

Finally, to our dream team of contributors, who brought this book to colorful life. You inspire me with your brilliant stories and ferocious talent. Lucky me. Luckier readers.